THE SHARKS

OF

LAKE NICARAGUA

THE SHARKS

OF

LAKE NICARAGUA

—

True Tales of Adventure, Travel, and Fishing

—

Randy Wayne White

THE LYONS PRESS

All of these stories, in shorter or edited forms, appeared in *Outside* magazine between the years 1987 and 1997. The author is much indebted to Larry Burke, Mark Bryant, Donovan Webster, and Hampton Sides of *Outside* for their advice and steadfast support.

Printed inCanada

10 9 8 7 6 5 4 3 2 1

Library of Congress Cataloging-in-Publication Data
White, Randy Wayne.
The sharks of Lake Nicaragua: true tales of adventure, travel, and fishing / Randy Wayne White.
p.   cm.
ISBN 1-58574-175-2(pb)   ISBN 1-55821-904-8
1. White, Randy Wayne—Journeys.   2. Ecotourism.   3. Voyages and travels.   4. Sharks—Nicaragua—Managua, Lake.
5. Travelers—United States—Biography.   I. Title.
G226.W48A3   1999
910.4—dc21   98-55425
CIP

I went to the woods because I wished to live deliberately, to front only the essential facts of life, and see if I could not learn what it had to teach, and not, when I came to die, discover that I had not lived.

—Henry David Thoreau
Walden

When I was very young and the urge to be someplace was on me, I was assured by mature people that maturity would cure this itch. When years described me as mature, the remedy prescribed was middle age. In middle age I was assured that greater age would calm my fever, and now that I am fifty-eight perhaps senility will do the job. Nothing has worked. In other words, I don't improve, in further words, once a bum always a bum.

—John Steinbeck
Travels with Charlie

"I like Third World countries. They're fun."

—Sighurdhr Tomlinson, to his friend Marion Ford

Contents

With love, respect and admiration for my son,

LEE W. WHITE,

upon his graduation from high school—

a great Third World travel partner, a gifted navigator, waterman,

and a good man to have at your side in a tough spot.

Introduction

As I write this, I am sitting at the helm of a forty-four-foot Thompson trawler, moored across the Sound, upriver from Tarpon Bay Marina, Sanibel Island, Florida, where I was once a fishing guide. It's late, nearly midnight. Beyond the frail incandescence of this wheelhouse is a van Gogh seascape: swirling stars and corridors of light on moving water. I can feel tide beneath the hull; can hear it currenting around pilings, drawn by a vacant moon. During my fishing-guide years—a time when many of the stories in this book were written—we would have described similar water as "sharky." To be sharky, water must be sufficiently dark and volatile to attract predators. It must demonstrate the potential to shield that which is unknown and may be dangerous. I like the idea that water which flows beneath this boat may well travel downriver, across Pine Island Sound, and end up in Tarpon Bay. I love the possibility that water which was once in Tarpon Bay—water upon which I fished—is, after several years of tidal influence, now moving among the mangrove feeder creeks of places I've been: Havana Harbor or the Chagres River in Panama or up the San Juan into one of the most remote places on earth, Lake Nicaragua. I also love the image of sharks, sharks inhabiting some far-off sea place, cruising water that was once home to me and my marina buddies at Tarpon Bay. There are no gates out there. More than one of my old clients heard me say that, and it's true.

No gates, you bet. All coastal places are more intimately linked to the wider world because of their connection to the sea. Ironically, though, it wasn't until I'd traveled the wider world that I began to understand that, as predators go, sharks do not compare to the dark creatures of our own construction. Bull sharks—an aggressive species found worldwide as well as in Lake Nicaragua—demonstrate a predatory indifference that borders on the existential, yet they seem pristine beings after dealing with the Third World's withering poverty or the new fascism of Political Correctness or the political imperatives that impose war upon children in small countries.

There are a lot of sharky places out there. There're a lot of dark things cruising.

This book deals with a few dark things, many bright things, and one interesting bullfrog. It consists of stories and essays, all variations on a theme. The theme is adventure-travel, a modern term for a pursuit that is older than tramp steamers, older than the Orient Express.

Adventure-travel ranges too far afield to be easily defined. That's why it confounds the bureaucratic jargon that herds and sanitizes more accommodating pastimes.

This century's final, nervous decade is repelled by people or pastimes that do not fit into a slot. Adventure-travel is the antithesis of these solemn times. That's one reason those of us who do it like it. I said that adventure-travel is difficult to define, which is true, but its description can at least be refined, and I'll try: Adventure-travel is any activity used as a conduit to observe, share, enjoy, suffer, encounter, or experience that which is outside the boundaries of one's own day-to-day life. You don't have to go to Thailand or Central America to be an adventure-traveler, but you can. And it's probably better not to have a specific goal, but there are no requirements about that, either. "Boundaries" is the operative word here; real, implied, or imagined, if your body or mind crosses a boundary, you are doing it.

Because we are the progeny of explorers and other hell-bent boundary crossers, adventure-travel comes naturally to an American, though a lot of Americans I meet won't believe it. The prospect of solo travel outside this country makes them edgy—an irony I once found perplexing, but now I think I understand. Pay close attention to the national media for a month, and you'll come to believe that the world dislikes Americans. Study the media for a year, and you'll come to the conclusion that the world has good reason. Name a sinister event, any social or environmental outrage, and there will be no shortage of editorials pointing the finger of blame squarely at ourselves. For people prone to self-predation, guilt is the new banner of American nationalism. It's being waved with baffling glee by New Age cloneites who apparently revel in self-flagellation and seldom miss an opportunity to declare their shame. The message becomes tiresome: The world hates Americans and we Americans deserve it.

Know what? That hasn't been my experience. Indeed, the opposite is true. Even traveling through such unlikely places as Cambodia, Nicaragua, Panama, and Cuba, I've been received warmly, even joyously, when my home port was made known.

"American?"

"Yeah, from America."

"Ho! An American!"

That word, "American," is usually spoken by outsiders with strange anticipation, as if, at any moment, they expect me to do something unusual or entertaining. Credit the movies, credit our history, I don't know or care, but it's true: People I've met around the world love Americans. If this country is hated, I'm convinced that most of that hatred comes from within, but neurotic dilettantes and naive goofs are beyond the purview—or understanding—of this book.

Generally, Americans are liked—of that I have no doubt. But as to the specifics of why we are liked or of how we are perceived, I don't even pretend to understand. The preconceptions are varied and sometimes a little startling. One example: A few years ago, on my way to Australia, I laid over in Fiji for several days. Each afternoon, I put on running shoes and jogged the streets of Suva, the capital city. Fiji lies between the equator and the Tropic of Capricorn, so it is brutally hot—a terrible place to run at midday. But hardship is no stranger to an adventure-traveler. Also, I was loony with jet lag and running gave me something to do while waiting for the beer locker to open at my hotel. So I ran each day and, each day, concerned strangers would stop their cars and ask polite questions before offering me a ride. Why was I running in this heat? Was I ill? Had I recently suffered a head wound?

I became accustomed to the inquiries, so was not surprised when a tiny East Indian man pulled off the road, stepped from his car and called to me, "Sir, would you prefer to ride?"

I said nope, I was just fine, thank you.

"Ah! You are an American, then?"

I nodded that I was.

Then, without preamble, the man hurried to my side and, while shaking my hand, said, "Thank God I've met you! I've just been married, and you will know. Please tell me: What can a man do to cure premature satisfaction?"

Some people say that America no longer inspires hope around the world? What nonsense! My reply to this desperate man wasn't equal to the pride he had fired in me. I said, "That's right, you guys don't play baseball in Fiji, do you?"

Being touched by a stranger's faith is not uncommon for an American traveler. It is part of the adventure-travel experience. The borders of that experience are limited only by one's disinclination to get off one's duff and try something, anything, new. A careful, monotonous life, in its way, is predacious. It feeds upon that singular human spark in us all which is brave hearted and unique. Personally, I'd rather swim with sharks. There are far darker, more sinister things out there cruising. . . .

RANDY WAYNE WHITE
Aboard the M/V Sea Gator
Fort Myers Yacht Basin
November 1998

ONE

DANGEROUS GAMES

Fighter Pilots USA

Here is why I recruited my friend, the Kumquat King, as an aerial combat opponent: Through a cagey gambit of equivocation and crawfishing, I had, for months, been dodging commitments to visit the F-16 jocks at Fighter Pilots USA. But even a cheap calendar can weather the most skillful lie, so inevitably, I knew, I would have to climb into the cockpit of a fighter plane and lay my lunch on the line.

Of course, a brochure produced by this private flying school presented a rosier view of the experience: "We offer the ultimate in high-speed, high-thrill air-combat maneuvering in a fighter aircraft at approximately 250 miles per hour. It is not a simulator. You fly the airplane . . . in numerous aerial dogfight engagements with an opponent. You do not need experience or a pilot's license . . . only a willingness to soar!"

Just reading the damn thing caused my hands to shake. True, not having a pilot's license made me half qualified, but, otherwise, I was conditionally indigent. Soaring is not something I do, willingly or otherwise—not because I lack courage, but because I suffer an affliction known as sympathetic ocular/auditory response, an esoteric distemper vague in its origins and humiliating in its symptoms: If bounced around in an airplane, my eyes begin to water, so that it appears as if I am weeping while I upchuck.

Yet, it was destined. Because my work required it, I would go to Fighter Pilots USA headquarters in Kissimmee, Florida (it abuts Disney World), and there be assigned to my host F-16 fighter pilot. I would be issued a flight suit, helmet, and parachute. During the morning ground school, I would learn the principles of air combat. I would be briefed on the safety features of the Marchetti fighter trainer my host and I would fly, and I would learn how to use the plane's fixed gun-sight visual tracking system. Then the hellish conclusion: We would take the Marchetti to six thousand feet where, at the controls, I would engage my opponent (a student in a second Marchetti) in a dogfight gumbo of loopty-loops, frenzied rolls, and high G-force climbs, plinking away at each other with 20-mm cannon. Worse, the whole business would be recorded by an in-cockpit video system so that, later, I would have to explain patiently to all viewers why, while holding a gun stick in one hand and a courtesy bag in the other, I was also sobbing.

All of this was mandated, so ordained; a fixed equation—as a professional adventurer, I know about these things. The lone x-factor was my opponent, and it was here I decided to try to exercise some control. Fighter Pilots USA attracted an enthusiastic clientele of men and women who, like me, had little or no flight training but who, unlike me, actually wanted to experience air combat. I didn't mind being blasted out of the sky, but I dreaded the prospect of being herded into any kind of unsettling evasive maneuvers by some gung-ho yupster. No, I wanted an opponent who shared my sensibilities and my pure love of standing on solid ground.

Which is why I thought of my friend, Bob Morris, the Kumquat King. Morris is known as the Kumquat King because he is the institutor of Orlando's strangest parade, the Queen Kumquat Sashay. Each November, a hundred thousand spectators turn out to watch a bizarre promenade of costumed outlanders; a troop that includes The Marching Dead Elvis Impersonators, The Hubble Telescope Repair Team, The World's Greatest Accordion Player and His Bimbo, along with a supporting cast of quirky thousands. A blindfolded Morris chooses a queen at random from the crowd ("Only rule is she has to be a redhead"). One year, the grand marshal was a cockroach. Traditionally, Morris is chauffeured along at the end of this aberration, tossing kumquats to the masses. ("That's the worst part—people throw the kumquats back at me, and it really hurts.")

Psychologically, Morris clearly had the right stuff. His approach to air combat would be as finicky and unconventional as my own. Also, like me, he was a husband and father with plenty of reasons to live. Finally, as a columnist for the *Orlando Sentinel*, he, too, was being pressured to go through the Fighter Pilots USA school.

"I keep putting them off, because I hate to fly," Morris had confided. "But I won't have to go. My editors will forget about it."

But they didn't forget. One evening Morris called to lament, "Can you believe it? They're making me do it!"

I wasn't the least bit surprised. Posing as an indignant reader, I had telephoned Morris's paper more than once to chide, "What, your reporters ain't got the vinegar to do that fighter pilot thing?"

Three weeks later, Morris and I met in the parking lot outside the airport offices of Fighter Pilots USA to negotiate a secret strategy.

"None of that dive-bomb business," Morris suggested. "In the parade, when my float goes down hill fast? It makes my stomach feel funny."

I assented, adding, "And no rolls. Even if the pilots try to make us roll, no rolls. I hate to roll."

"Just standing up fast makes me dizzy," Morris said agreeably. "And how about this: No quick turns. If you don't turn fast, I won't have to turn fast."

I said, "Check."

"You know what we ought to do?" Morris had obviously been giving this a lot of thought. "What we ought to do is go up there, you shoot me once, I'll shoot you once, then we tell them to get us the hell back down on the ground. No swooping, no soaring—ten minutes in the air, tops."

Which is exactly why I recruited my friend, the Kumquat King, as my aerial combat opponent.

The first hint of change in the Kumquat King's attitude came shortly after we entered the neat modular offices of Fighter Pilots USA. We had already been introduced to our hosts, Timothy "Toast" DesMarais and Kim "Iceman" Heishman, ramrod-straight F-16 jocks who, like every fighter pilot I have ever met, manifested confidence and competence while also demonstrating a bedrock appreciation for all things funny, bawdy, fast, or high tech. To Morris I had confided, "Even if the worst happens, we'll be safe with these guys."

Morris seemed unconvinced, but a few minutes later I heard him call from the pilot's ready room, "Hey, take a look at me, man!"

He stepped out wearing an olive drab flight suit, a silver fighter pilot's helmet tucked under his arm, swaggering a little as he demonstrated all the neat zipper pockets. "It's strange," he said, "but just putting this thing on makes me feel . . . different. *Better*, somehow. Ya know, when you think about it, this is a pretty interesting thing we're doing."

It got worse. During our classroom session on the principles of air combat, Morris not only asked questions, he made notes. Then, when we split into groups for private strategy briefings (Morris was teamed with Heishman; me with DesMarais), I stuck my ear to the door and overheard Morris say, "All I want to do is shoot Randy's butt out of the sky!"

My God, what had happened to the man? Had he taken DesMarais's classroom "No Guts, No Glory" speech to heart? Or maybe he had been whacked on the beezer by one too many kumquats. No telling. All I knew was, Morris had gone through a strange, inexplicable transformation. Our secret peace accord had hit the skids—but the bastard wasn't going to double-cross me and get away with it.

I didn't yet have a gun, but both F-16 pilots had said (implied, actually) that psychological warfare was perfectly acceptable in air combat, and I immediately went to work on Toast DesMarais.

To Toast, I said, "Morris loves that flight suit he's wearing. Even if it does have an American flag sewn on the shoulder."

Toast was sitting at a desk, checking weather reports. "Yeah, they're great suits"—but then he paused and looked up. "Hey . . . wait a minute. What does Morris have against the American flag?"

"Are you kidding? You don't know about the guy's politics?" I made a gesture of dismissal. "Look, forget I said anything about Hanoi Bob. That's all water under the bridge."

"*Hanoi Bob?*"

To Toast, I said, "Now I'm sorry I even brought it up."

As we walked outside to strap on our parachutes, I edged up to Iceman Heishman and said, "It's darn nice of you to fly with Morris—especially after what he called you back in the ready room."

Iceman said, "Yeah, Bob's a great guy"—but then he stopped and said, "Huh?"

"You didn't hear him?" Well, he was probably just joking. I mean, to call a guy like you a right-wing, bald-headed, war-mongering sonofabitch—"

Iceman tapped his fists together. "He called me *bald?*"

Tough stuff, but psychological warfare ("psychic ops," we call it) is not a game for the fainthearted. As it turned out, I should have started earlier and been even tougher because, once we had been strapped into our respective aircraft, the Kumquat King abandoned all pretense of control. The left seat joystick of a Marchetti fighter trainer is equipped with an intercom button and a weapons trigger. Call "Gun, gun gun!" into the intercom, squeeze the trigger, and the firing of 20-mm cannon is simulated by a piercing electronic whine heard in a flight helmet's earphones. Taxiing out onto the runway, I heard Morris shoot a perfectly innocent Cessna landing on the tarmack. Then he shot a DC-3 outside its hangar. The Sea World blimp (a gigantic Shamu) was tethered at the edge of Kissimmee Airport, and Morris shot that, too.

To Toast, sitting at my right, I said, "Lordy, he just blasted the whale!"

Toast was chuckling into his headset. "Yeah, and now he's giving you the bird."

It was true. Inside the canopy bubble, I could see Morris pressing his rude digit to the glass, a maniacal expression on his face. To Toast, I said, "I don't want to upset you, Colonel, but he's aiming that finger at you."

Toast DesMarais said, "Oh, he is, is he?" and punched the Marchetti down the runway to flight.

It was war.

To watch the videotape of the series of dogfights that ensued is, frankly, humiliating. On the ground, I think most people who know me would agree that I am unpretentiously confident; a trained athlete and adventurer who keeps a cool head even in tinderbox situations. Not so in the air—according to the cockpit flight camera anyway. The tape shows me popping my chewing gum like some nervous bus-stop floozy while spouting the kind of mindless non sequiturs more easily associated with, say, Gomer Pyle on some very serious speed.

I say things like, "Ooooh-h-h-h HA! Jesus frogs!" And "Tip-p-i-i-i-ing . . . tip-p-i-i-ing . . . yes, yes . . . we are UPSIDE DOWN!"

During a segment that captures a particularly gut-wrenching high G-force climb, I can watch myself as I scream, "Urine? URINE! My God, I think urine is coming out of . . . out of my . . . OUT OF MY NOSE!"

Which is why I do not like to watch the tape of those dog-fights. Also, the tape makes me queasy for, beyond my helmeted head, the lakes and fields and clouds of central Florida spin ceaselessly—a stunning testament to what I endured that day.

But I didn't get queasy during the flight. Not once; didn't even come close. I was too busy trying to evade the Kumquat King so that I could get him in my gun sights. Amazing, but true. Something else that is amazing is, after my first tentative banks and rolls during our practice sessions, I began to enjoy it. Also true. Nothing I have ever experienced in my life—downhill ski-ing, kayaking, rafting rapids, climbing, falling down hills, bal-looning, marathon running, mountain biking, or being lost in the jungle, *nothing*—has ever come close to matching the adrena-line rush and emotional intensity of that one hour of mock air combat.

Not that I realized it at the time. Pure terror does not tolerate conflicting sentiment. I flew terrified, and I stayed terrified until I got back on the ground again. Which may explain why Morris got the jump on me in our first two engagements. He rolled hard over at each start ("No rolls. Promise!"), then tried to put his lift vector on my tail through a series of high and low yo-yos—a strategy that will mean nothing to the layman, but is chillingly descriptive to us fighter pilots. But each time, with Toast coolly calling out advice, I stiff-armed the bastard into resignation. The result: two fights, two draws.

I was willing to leave it at that. Storm pods had been building around us, and I was amenable to landing early—in fact, I suggested it. But Morris, using the radio to chide and denigrate ("I've always got time for a quickie!") goaded me into a third and final combat. Double-crossing me was one thing, but then to insist on prolonging the agony was madness, and I had had a bellyful. This time, I rolled on the break, ascended to gain speed, then pulled out in a high G-turn with cannon blazing. For long seconds, it seemed (only microseconds, according to the video gun camera) I held the Kumquat King dead in my sights, calling, as I did, "Die, hippie! Die!"

A plume of smoke bloomed out of my enemy's aircraft . . . it was destroyed; the war was over . . . and, better yet, Morris puked shortly thereafter.

That's my favorite part on the video.

Snow Hounds from Hell

My sled had flipped, and I was being dragged by five speed-crazy sled dogs; dragged over hill and dale, maybe being dragged to death—or worse, to Nome, which was more than a thousand miles away and the natural destination of beasts trained for long-distance races such as the Iditarod.

But I couldn't let go of the sled. Only minutes before, I had been told that, above all else, rookie mushers must remember to never, ever let go of their sled. The reason was simple: Sled dogs love to run and hate to stop, so, even if they lose a driver, they will keep right on running until they get to wherever they think they are supposed to go. And they will get there hours or days or even weeks ahead of the fool who lost his grip and had to crawl home through butt-deep snow, eating twigs and glove leather just to survive.

In Alaska, the expression "He let go of the sled" may not be common, but, when used, it summarizes the flaky or irrational behavior of a garden variety of goons, goofs, and other low-rent travelers who, often as not, come from the lower forty-eight states.

No cowardly epitaphs for this mainlander, though. No sir. Call it pride, call it a sense of honor, call it quiet courage—but, when my sled flipped, I refused to let go. True, the hood of my parka had become tangled in the harness and I couldn't let go, but this is precisely the kind of situation where quiet courage goes so unheralded. Never mind that I was being dragged on my belly, head banging up and down over limb and ice mogul, arms and legs thrown akimbo as they clawed for purchase. I still had the presence of mind to take charge of a difficult situation:

"Whoa! Whoa, damn you! Whoa when I yell whoa!"

But many sled dogs cannot run and hear at the same time—at least, that was my experience. Not that I had much experience. It was all new to me because it was my first try at dog mushing (as it is called by the indoctrinated). Frankly, I had never had much interest in mushing; indeed, had never even thought of mushing until it was suggested that I travel to Alaska prior to the Iditarod, take a lesson or two in the sport, and report back for the benefit of other would-be mushers. Is it fun? Is it safe? Does it take much skill? Is it hard to learn? Is it painful for the animals? Are the drivers really athletes? When an ice slab loosens one's teeth, do the dogs frenzy at the smell of blood? All reasonable questions—and who better to answer them than a professional outdoorsman such as myself?

There are those who live for adventure, to whom fear is a chaperone, danger a mistress; a wild breed that thrives in the

rarefied air of outdoor peril—and why editors continue to con-
fuse me with such twisted granola stuffers is anybody's guess. But
dog mushing seemed benign in comparison to some of the luna-
cies for which they have volunteered me. How hard could it be?

"Not that hard," my instructor, Dan Seavey of Seward, Alaska,
told me.

Of course. Where was the challenge in standing on a sled
while animals pulled you?

"Oh, mushing can be a challenge all right," Seavey insisted,
then added cryptically, "but the trail might be the best way for
you to learn that."

Maybe—though I was in no position to debate dogs or sleds
with Seavey because, for the last three decades, they have been
his passions. He taught dog mushing as a high school teacher,
raced and placed in the first two Iditarods, and, in 1983, was
appointed by the Secretary of the Interior to serve on the
Iditarod Trail Advisory Council. Now, at fifty-four, he continues
to raise and train dogs, and teaches mushing as co-owner of
Trails North Tours. Trails North specializes in arranging Iditarod
and other Alaskan tours for nonmushers as well as would-be
mushers, and it was Seavey, along with his partner Whitey Van
Deusen, who offered to give me a two-day sledding primer.

I met with Seavey and Van Deusen at their adjoining homes
and training grounds just outside Kenai Fjords National Park on
the Kenai Peninsula—a place of extraordinary scenery and
wildlife. I was given a tour of the sled-building shop, its rafters
crisscrossed with sweet-smelling strips of cured hickory, oak, and
ash. Then I was introduced to the dogs.

Mushers, as might be expected, take their dogs seriously. They love to talk about famous dogs of the past and their personal favorites; about qualities of various breeds and the benefits of crossbreeding. I am a dog and cat fancier and have a good eye, I think, for animals that are well cared for and happy in their homes. But the sled dogs I met weren't just happy, they were ecstatic, or so they seemed, as Seavey made the rounds, scratching ears and calling their names. What surprised me most was that the dogs were so friendly. I expected foul-humored creatures, quick to growl and quicker to fight, but, in my travels around Alaska, I didn't meet a single rank sled dog. Indeed, they are among the sweetest animals I have ever encountered.

"Most sled dogs are people oriented," Seavey explained. "That's a preferred characteristic. Some of these dogs are third and fourth generation from my original team and, while each dog has his own personality, some of the traits are real consistent. They get to be like kids if you spend enough time with them. A few of my dogs are descended from the old Leonhard Seppala Siberian line." (The modern Iditarod commemorates the route taken by Seppala and others who, in 1925, relayed diphtheria medicine to Nome and stopped an epidemic that had already killed five children.) "It's that kind of tradition and heritage those of us who work to promote dog mushing are trying to preserve."

According to Seavey, most good sled dogs are a cross between Siberian husky and what mushers call "village dogs," or local crossbreeds. That mix, which is called "Alaskan husky," is not recognized as a separate breed, though sledders insist that it is. If you don't like dogs, you won't like mushing—that is one of the rare absolutes in sport. "Ninety percent of mushing," said Seavey, "is caring for your team, training them, making sure they get the best treatment, the best care."

Probably ninety percent of the expense, too. You can buy a used stanchion sled for a couple of hundred dollars, and you can buy a pretty good pup, according to most mushers I spoke with, for two hundred to five hundred dollars. (You need at least three dogs to get into the sport.) But grown, trained team dogs will cost a thousand dollars or more, and a prime lead dog could cost ten thousand. Add to that the cost of high-quality feed (every musher seems to have her or his own favorite and sometimes secret formula) plus vet bills, and it can get expensive.

"Mushing can become as demanding and complicated as you want to make it," Seavey told me. "Basically, though, it's not hard and it's a heck of a lot of fun. The dogs are pretty user friendly, and the only thing the beginner has to remember is don't let go of the sled—and don't be afraid."

Right. And what was there to fear? Dog sledding didn't involve heights, caves, rapids, waterfalls, sharks, car rental clerks, or border guards—so there was absolutely no reason to be afraid.

Or so I thought until I had harnessed my dogs and stood on the sled runners for the first time.

Here was one reason to be afraid. Standing on sled runners behind five fresh huskies is, to the uninitiated, the probable equivalent of awaiting takeoff in one of those Big Daddy Don Garlitz–type rail dragsters. Ahead is the trail—much of it downhill—and the way the dogs yammer and lunge, anxious to get started, implies the unavoidable: Sooner than you wish, you will be traveling a hell of a lot faster than you want.

Seavey and I had loaded ten dogs into his truck (every dog in his kennel was wild to go) and we drove along Resurrection Bay to Mile Zero at Iditarod Trailhead Park. (The original Iditarod Trail connected the freeze-proof seaport of Seward on Resurrection Bay with Nome nearly one thousand miles away. Today, the famous sled race begins in Anchorage and ends in Nome, but the Bureau of Land Management has set aside nearly 2,300 miles of wilderness pathway as Iditarod National Historic Trail.) The day was clear, the temperature only slightly below freezing, so Seavey explained that we would make a lot of stops to rest the dogs.

"When it's warm like this," he said, "they can wear themselves out pretty quick."

I, for one, hoped so.

After Seavey explained the parts of the sled to me (basket, runners, shoes, handles, and much more) and demonstrated how to harness the dogs (a neck lead that connects to a trace line that runs to a bridle) he showed me what I instantly recognized as truly important equipment: the snow brake and the snow anchor. The snow brake is a steel spike that the driver can force down into the snow with his feet and thus slow the dogs. The snow anchor is just that: a metal drain attached to a rope that one may bury just as one might set an anchor to hold a boat.

"You shouldn't have to use either one much," Seavey said.

Well, let him think that if he wanted.

I buried both the anchor and the brake in the snow, then busied myself harnessing my dogs. As I said, sled dogs are sweet animals, and they are fun to watch because their personalities often signature their assigned positions on the sled. The team dogs like to wrestle and lope like pups while the lead dogs go their own way, sniffing, standing apart as they lend great dignity to the determinations of whereupon to pee. Most mushers I spoke with agreed that good sled dogs usually aren't huge (rarely more than sixty pounds), but they are tremendously strong and have great endurance.

But even a nonmusher like myself could have anticipated these qualities. What I didn't anticipate was how much the dogs love to pull a sled. And they do. There is no mistaking their enthusiasm: They run to the trace, not away from it, then stand patiently to be harnessed—even if by a bumbling amateur. But once harnessed, look out. By the time I got my fifth and final dog tied in, I knew that no combination of brake and anchor was strong enough to hold these brutes. So I jumped on the back of the sled and applied my full weight to the brake, but even that wasn't enough to keep the sled from being pulled forward.

Seavey's team was already harnessed and ready. "They want to go!" he yelled, then he was away on the trail—an event that whipped my team into a yapping, straining frenzy. Carefully, carefully, I reached out to pull the snow anchor . . . and that's the last unblurred remembrance I have of the events that followed. There was the sensation of speed . . . of insane, careening neck-break speed . . . and flying tears—dear God, I was crying— or maybe it was just the wind contorting my face and creating tears; yeah, that was it. My team wanted to catch Seavey's team, and no power on Earth could stop them.

I made no effort to steer or yell commands. It would have been futile. And if I fell off that sled, I knew spring would return before those damn dogs did. I stood crouched on the thin runners, holding on for dear life. It seemed we descended that hill at a speed in excess of a hundred miles an hour, though perhaps it wasn't quite that fast. ("Probably about fifteen miles per hour," Seavey would guess later—an absurd understatement.)

Then the trail leveled out. Consciousness gradually returned, as did my senses.

The dogs had been barking madly, but now they were focused and silent. Buster was my lead dog, my swing dogs were Raven and Zidza, and my wheel dogs were Spud and Spike. The five of them trotted in synch through a cavern of snow forest, the pads of their feet and the sled runners creating a trickling hiss, like running water. That's what I remember best about those first minutes: the hush of an Alaskan winter; of being spirited, like wind, through a formidable void, a woodland tunnel of white, and the world was quiet, quiet.

I liked it. I liked mushing as well as any sport I have ever tried. The dogs, the silence, the speed, the mobility, the unity, I liked it all. True, I flipped the sled three times before I realized that a driver doesn't have to stand immobile on the runners. He can (indeed, must) get off and run sometimes—which makes mushing an endurance sport for dog and driver alike. True, I once broke sledding's cardinal rule and let go of the sled—but I had to, because my hands refused to hold on to the grips when my face and chest hit that elm tree.

But when we finally caught the dogs, and I got back aboard my sled, I liked mushing no less. In truth, I liked it more.

Antiterrorist Driving School

Angel tells us that if we don't rally the nerve to explore our automotive limits, the bad guys will nail us at the choke point and pop us on the X. They'll stop us, box us, then smoke us like cheap cigars.

"Ka-ba-OOHM!" emphasizes Angel, a man who delights in imagery as well as interpretive sound effects.

As we have already learned, a "choke point" is an unavoidable route that one's car must travel. The "X" is a spot where one is most likely to be shot, rocketed, or (Angel's favorite) bombed by terrorists or similar scum. "*Sputnik* city," Angel explains. "We're talking roadkill."

I don't doubt that he is correct—and, if I did doubt him, I wouldn't admit it. Angel, though likable and articulate, resembles a Tasmanian devil reanimated as a descendent of Pancho Villa. When Angel talks, people interested in avoiding death by terrorism listen. He is an expert on explosives, tactical weaponry, evasive driving, and other oddments useful if one is planning to invade a small country.

"Or if you're planning to leave the house," insists Angel. "These days, no matter where you go, there's a threat of terrorism or criminal attack. You could be whacked at any time. Like the people pulled from their cars and beaten during the L.A. riots. Or the German tourists in Miami. In country or out. If you travel, you're at risk."

A desire not to be whacked is why I have enrolled in BSR Inc.'s Executive Security Training course held at Summit Point, West Virginia. I travel a lot. I spend an inordinate amount of time driving foreign cars, lost in foreign cities. True, it has been my experience that people around the world are uniformly pleasant if not downright hospitable. But there are exceptions, and BSR Inc. has the slide show to prove it: image after image of human carrion created by political dysfunctional and other terrorist groups such as The Red Brigade and Aldo Moro.

"You never know," joked Matthew Croke, Director of Training, prior to his colorful introductory lecture on assassinations. "Terrorists could mistake you for someone important."

If they do, the bastards will have only themselves to blame: The experts at BSR don't exactly graduate pantywaists. In my four days at this school I will learn how to use an automobile as a weapon. I will learn how to execute forward and reverse emergency turns. I will learn how to analyze surveillance operations and detect car bombs. I will learn how to ram cars off the highway, and keep my own car on the highway while being fired upon by attackers during high-speed pursuit scenarios. This is no namby-pamby theorist's school, either (though classroom work is part of it). At BSR, students experience tire-screaming, real-life, hands-on-the-wheel situations not suitable for the faint of heart.

In short, here I will learn all I need to know to survive an assault by terrorists or rush hour in places like Baghdad or Chicago. If James Bond had to choose a driving school, it would be BSR Inc. It is the real-life choice of the United States Department of State, the Department of Defense, various specialized military teams, as well as a garden variety of clandestine organizations, many of which are conveniently located only two hours away in Washington D.C. As a result, all BSR instructors have security clearance, so students benefit from up-to-the-minute data on terrorism.

Where else can you sit in a room decorated with framed quotes of international murderers and learn how easy it is to make a car bomb using a Ping-Pong ball, a dab of super glue, and a third ingredient that Angel is judicious enough not to reveal?

"The point is," he says, standing in front of his display case of homemade bombs, "that it is easy to blow up a car. What we want to teach you is attack recognition; how to be a tough target."

Angel refers us to a Baader-Meinhof slogan on the wall: *When you are hungry, it is foolish to hunt a tiger when there are plenty of sheep to be had,* before adding, "That's one of the keys. Don't be passive. Be a tiger. If you're attacked, outrun them. If you can't outrun them, we'll teach you how to lay a little Goodyear on them."

The thought of that obviously pleases Angel, for he grins before summation: "In other words, make the bastards pick on somebody weaker than you."

I am all for bad guys picking on someone weaker than me; the nobility of mankind has been reduced by crime and terrorism and, in a tight spot, my own nobility puckers accordingly. The problem, unfortunately, is that it is unlikely that terrorists will be able to find someone—anyone—who is an easier automotive target than I. This is not a play for sympathy; hell, for many years I have taken pride in it. Fast drivers? I think they're dopes. Just like back in high school, squealing tires and revving engines are the pubescent cries of mullocks desperate for attention. That, plus cars scare me. I admit it. Indeed, I have a bedrock horror of ending up the victim in some roadside tableau: plasma bags and hubcaps amid the ditchweed, all because of some pimply-headed geek or a bored taxi driver in a fast car. Is there a more adolescent way to die? Is there a dumber way?

But as Brent Hollida, my own personal driving instructor, tells me, "Any idiot can press a gas pedal to the floor. That's not what this school is about. There is craftsmanship to high-speed evasive driving. That's what we're here to teach you."

That BSR has reduced the craft to science cannot be questioned. Ten to twelve hours a day, the course syllabus alternates between classroom lectures on automotive theory interrupted by high-speed thrills and chills driving the school's Chevy Caprice police cruisers in which our instructors urge us to use the 350-horsepower engines to full advantage.

For me, there are more chills than thrills. The first time Hollida demonstrates a high-speed lap around BSR's beautiful two-mile, ten-turn road course, I climb out of the car with my teeth clicking like dice at a Reno crap table. Had we really entered that 90-degree turn doing 115 miles per hour?

"You'll be doing the same thing in a few days," Brent assures me. "In a life-or-death situation, you need to know how to get all you can out of your vehicle. Don't worry—you'll learn all the necessary skills a step at a time."

Worried? When it comes to cars, I was born worried. But Brent is determined to teach me the skills, anyway.

Set off by itself in the scenic wooded hills of eastern West Virginia, the BSR training center is a fascinating place. Along with the road track, the 472-acre facility offers an irrigated skid pad, nine target or combat shooting ranges, an explosives range, a forty-foot rappel tower, and plenty of drop zones for parachute jumps. It does not surprise me that several of my fellow students, though thoroughly pleasant guys, do not wear name tags. ("It's best not to ask about my occupation," more than one told me.) Nor was it surprising that, yesterday morning, most of them performed better than I on the skid pad—though BSR Inc. now welcomes students from the private sector, I am the only nonprofessional in this course. Two pupils and one instructor per car, we wheeled out onto an asphalt doughnut soaked by sprinklers and, there, accelerated until our vehicles were forced to spin crazily. At least, that's what the other students did. Brent finally lost patience with my tentativeness and put his foot on the accelerator while I steered.

"When the car begins to slide," he told me over and over, "shift your eyes to a positive goal and steer toward it. Remember: Steering takes priority over braking! If you look at only what you don't want to hit, you almost certainly *will* hit it."

The technique is called positive ocular-response driving—the validity of which I no longer doubt after ramming many things that couldn't move and a couple of things that should have.

I did better in the threshold-breaking exercises. Doing one hundred miles per hour, Brent would suddenly yell, "Brake right!" and I would mash the left pedal with enthusiasm, ever alert to the numbing steering wheel that warns of locked brakes, all the while trying to weave my way through a maze of plastic cones.

On the track this morning, however, high-speed pursuit exercises (an "evolution," as the instructors call each drill) thrust my bumbling amateur status back to the fore. "You have to force yourself to go faster," Brent keeps telling me. "The only way you can learn a vehicle's limits is to explore the envelope. Remember, this is a life-or-death situation. You're running for your life."

Frankly, running for my life is something I've always believed I would be good at. But when I get behind the wheel of a car I just naturally take my foot off the accelerator when approaching a series of hairpin turns. Same with a hill—who the hell knows for certain what's waiting on the other side? By steeling myself, I can manage 110 miles per hour on the straightaway; I can skid into the first turn and drift through it bravely enough. But when confronted by a hill and a series of S-turns, I just can't make myself hold the accelerator to the floor.

"You have to push the limits," Brent keeps repeating. "Yours and the car's."

This course is not just about driving fast, and I find the lectures on the analysis of attacks by terrorists and criminals fascinating. Daily, we study how targets are selected, how attacks are planned, practiced, and deployed. By scrutinizing the details of well-known attacks, we learn how the attacks might have been avoided, or how victims might have saved themselves. Our instructors refer obliquely—never openly—to certain antiterrorist teams of which they seem to have some knowledge. And they also make inside jokes about their love of rental cars. ("Don't wear a BSR hat to the Hertz desk—they'll kick you out.")

The morning's evolution on vehicular evasive tactics will effectively demonstrate why that is so. After driving us to an open stretch of track, Brent tells a fellow student and me, "Attacks are most commonly initiated by a ruse: a faked accident or a broken-down car; some kind of roadblock that forces the target to stop on the X. Today, you'll learn three very effective ways to get off the X and flee the killing zone." Brent then shifts the car into drive, accelerates to about forty miles an hour . . . then locks the emergency brake while turning the wheel a quarter turn. Tires scream and the car revolves sickeningly before Brent releases the emergency brake and hits the gas: Amazingly, we are already traveling at speed in the opposite direction.

"That's sometimes called a boot turn," Brent explains, "named after the bootleggers who used it to outrun police. Think of it as a forward hundred-and-eighty-degree turn."

Brent then shifts into reverse and floors the accelerator, counting aloud, "Thousand one, thousand two, thousand three, thousand four," before removing his foot from the gas and spinning the steering wheel toward the empty lane: Just as quickly, the front end of the car swings around and we are traveling in the opposite direction. "That," he says, "is a J-turn. Think of it as a reverse hundred-and-eighty-degree turn."

We spend the next hour practicing the turns, and, when I finally start to get the hang of it, I, too, find myself eager to sign my next rental car contract. But we are not done for the day. We have one more evasive tactic to learn: barricade breaching. ("Think of it as ramming," says Brent.)

Angel takes charge of this evolution in which, student by student, we take turns crashing through a wrecked car that blocks the road. The key, says Angel, is to fake a stop by slowing to ten to fifteen miles per hour, then accelerating through the barricade. "Hit their tire with your tire! Make their car absorb the impact. Never brake!"

Intentionally crashing into another car goes against all instincts and that's doubly true of keeping one's foot on the gas throughout the collision. But with Angel looking on, yelling like some demented Sergeant Carter ("Move it! Move it! Move it!"), it's not as hard as one might think.

The final evolutions of the course include two graduate-level exercises. The first, held on the road track, consists of instructors ambushing us, chasing us, banging our bumpers at crazed speeds, and firing blanks at us while herding our cars toward roadblocks where those not delirious with fear are expected to react with the proper boot turn, J-turn, or ram. The second requires that students pile into a van and drive peacefully through the streets of nearby Winchester, Virginia, while pinpointing surveillants and where, exactly, terrorists plan to transform us into roadkill.

Guess which of the two evolutions I prefer.

Being spied upon is exciting. We spend four hours driving to and from our fictional workplaces, ever alert while traveling choke points, dutifully logging the physical description and license numbers of suspicious-looking people (surprisingly, sleepy little Winchester is awash with suspicious-looking people). We note suspected terrorists in Volvos and Cadillacs, jogging and guzzling wine, building fences, pushing baby carriages (one of the oldest terrorist tricks in the book), and rummaging through dumpsters. The bastards are everywhere—or so it seems to our paranoid group in the van.

Actually, most of our suspicions are wasted on ghosts (a code word for innocent citizenry), but we aren't always wrong. State Department agents (I think) are working in concert with us as a proactive antisurveillant squad, and once we have eliminated them from the list of cars and people tailing us, zoning in on the terrorists becomes easier. Feeling badly about my performance on the road track, I decide to try to demonstrate to my fellow students that I'm not a total putz by carefully analyzing the four pages of data in our log. My prediction: We will be attacked at the corner of Whittier Street and Amherst by two women and three men.

One hour later, that's exactly what happens: At the corner of Whittier and Amherst, a car pulls out as a roadblock, and we are attacked by two women and three men.

Impressed only slightly, my driving instructor will later comment, "Observation is a critical part of the game—but just be glad they didn't try to chase you."

Diving Nine

Florida treasure hunters are as common as Kansas wheat, so it is not surprising that I, because of my specialized knowledge and diverse aquatic skills, receive many requests for assistance from this peculiar wingnut fringe. Normally, I decline involvement. Just because some of these people can find their way across the state line doesn't mean they can find a sunken boat. But a few years ago I did get involved, which is probably why my attitude toward treasure hunters is jaundiced.

I was enlisted by a man who convinced me that he had located a World War I cargo ship that had carried pharmaceuticals, including, he said, several thousand vials of extremely valuable mercury. In those days, indicated treatment for syphilis included mercury injected directly up the urethra—a gruesome ordeal called "God's Revenge" by abstainers and similarly uninteresting people. The treasure hunter told me that ship and manifest had been lost to a German U-boat while en route to South America, and, to become wealthy, all we had to do was salvage the mercury. "Mercury floats," he said. "We free the vials from the crates and they'll bob to the surface like toy ducks."

In hindsight, I might have asked why the War Department was shipping mercury to Argentina when our randy doughboys were in France, but I didn't, which is why I ended up in one hundred twenty feet of water fanning sand away from what could have been crates of pharmaceuticals, but turned out to be crates of unexploded ordnance instead. If mercury was listed on the manifest, it was probably mercury fulminate, a chemical detonator, and not the medicinal mercury chloride—which, as I discovered later, would have been worthless, anyway. It was terrifying being down there with corroded seventy-year-old bombs and, while surfacing, I sustained myself during the long decompression stops with the pure joy I would take in thrashing that idiot treasure hunter if we ever made it back to shore.

Since then, as I said, my view has been jaundiced. So recently, when my friend Stout called me with another treasure-hunting scheme, I was quick to refuse.

"But you don't even have to go in the water," he pressed. "We just need you to stay on shore and watch for alligators. And the night watchman, of course."

Alligators? Night watchman? This was a fresh approach, and I decided to listen.

"You are an expert on alligators, aren't you?"

Actually, I am an expert on avoiding alligators, but when a compliment is offered, it is impolite to contest it.

"Expert?" I said. "Certainly. Everyone knows that."

"Then you're exactly the guy we need. And you'll get an equal share of the take."

Normally, treasure hunters, like film producers, talk in terms of "points of the net," so the whole thing was sounding better and better. Stout proceeded to tell me his scheme. Did I realize, he began, that there were more than five thousand golf courses in Florida? And did I realize that, each day, tens of thousands of very expensive golf balls were dinked into lakes by golfers who, because they are prissy by nature, don't bother to go in after them? Because of this, Stout said, retrieving golf balls was a hugely profitable business.

"There are people around who have made millions just diving for golf balls," Stout said. "A good quality ball costs two bucks or more new, and from forty cents to a buck used. And it's nothing for one diver to take a thousand balls from a single lake. Understand, people who run country clubs aren't dumb, so they contract out the salvage rights and get a percentage of the profits back from the divers. It's a very nice, neat business, which is why ball divers keep the whole thing hushed up. Why share a sweet deal like that?"

Several hundred dollars or more for a day's work—why, indeed? "So you've undercut those greedy spawn," I said, "and negotiated your own contract with a country club?"

Stout said, "Not yet. That's the next step, but first we need some operating capital. This is a very specialized kind of diving. Because of all the fertilizers and pesticides, golf course lakes are a kind of a chemical soup. You come out glowing, your chromosomes completely out of whack—unless you wear a full face mask and a dry suit. Total protection is imperative. But that kind of equipment is expensive, so to raise some cash we're going to dive a local golf course. At night."

"At night?" I repeated.

"The later the better."

Why didn't the man just come right out and say that he wanted me to help him pirate a country club? "Do you know what you're proposing?" I asked. "Felonious trespass, grand theft, not to mention probably breaking all acceptable standards of golf course etiquette. That's what you have in mind?"

"Exactly," Stout replied. "Just you and me and one other guy. We make one big score, then divvy the profits."

It sounded wonderful. "Tell me more," I said.

Stout explained that our partner (I'll call him Carlson) already had a dry suit, and he knew the business, so he would do the actual diving on our night assault. The two of them had thought long and hard about which of the dozens of local courses to hit, and had settled on an exclusive club called Royal Palm Beach View. "We want an upscale course," Stout said. "At a mobile-home-and-Chevy club, we'd get nothing but X-ed out Spauldings and range balls. Worthless. But Beach View is strictly Titleist and Dunlop trade. The trash cans there are stuffed with Perrier bottles and new ball wrappers. Carlson checked. Hell, they warm up with Top Flites and leave them for the riffraff. And here's the best thing: No one has ever dove the lakes. The place has never been salvaged. And do you want to know why?"

I already knew why: alligators. Located on a posh vacation island, Beach View was acrawl with gators because the island's nature-loving citizenry insisted that the club's lakes remain a kind of crocodilian breeding factory. Though not a golfer, I had once snuck onto the course to fly-cast for landlocked tarpon. The memory was terrible to recall. Each time I hooked a tarpon, alligators would converge on the fish in a horrible feeding frenzy: nothing but flying scales and slapping tails in a froth of red. That one experience was enough. I considered Royal Palm Beach View a genuinely dangerous place, and it was my own private suspicion that more vacationing Ohioans and New Yorkers had disappeared on that course than had been lost at Gettysburg.

Stout said, "You ever hear of El Dorado? Well, Beach View is the El Dorado of golf-ball hunters. They've been hitting preemo balls into those lakes for decades, and no one has ever—*ever*—gone in after them. Now the question is"—Stout's tone changed from ebullient to serious—"the question is, can you deal with the gators so it's safe for Carlson to get in the water?"

Safe? Just playing eighteen at Beach View was dangerous; attempting to dive it at night was insanity. "Does this guy Carlson have any dependents?" I asked.

"I don't think so. He's got a dry suit. That's all I need to know."

"We don't go in the water?"

"I'll wade around and mule balls out, and you'll stay on the bank as a kind of safety officer. Carlson says that we can expect to clear a thousand, maybe fifteen hundred bucks. Each. What do you think?"

Fifteen hundred dollars for one night's work—and all I had to do was stand on the bank. "In this case," I told my friend Stout, "I think the risk factor is perfectly acceptable."

Our first attempt to dive Beach View did not go well. When one imagines pirating a country club lake, one imagines the cheerful clink of golf balls being shoveled into buckets. One does not imagine first lugging tanks, fins, dive sacks and miscellaneous gear a mile or more from an innocuous parking spot, then at least another mile over midnight fairways where any fallen log might actually be a big bull gator on the prowl.

Carlson, it turned out, was a whiner. "Why do I have to go first?" he kept asking. "I'm the one going in the water. You guys should at least lead the way to the lake."

"As safety officer," I explained to him, "it's important I remain at the rear. If the worst happens, I need to be closest to the car so I can go for help."

But common sense couldn't dent Carlson's cowardly nature. He complained about having to carry his own gear, he griped about how hot it was inside his dry suit.

"Gad!" Stout finally snapped at him. "Just be thankful you've got some protection from the mosquitoes. They're eating me alive!"

It was true. Mosquitoes had found us in swarms. Not that Carlson was concerned. The man cared only for his own comfort and safety. But it was when we finally came to a lake that he demonstrated the degree of his self-absorption. I shined my small flashlight over the water's surface. It was a typical Florida golf course lake—longer than it was wide, with palm trees silhouetted at the edge. "See there?" I told Carlson. "Not a single gator. Their eyes glow at night, so it's easy to tell." I switched off the light, hoping my enthusiasm would be contagious. "Piece of cake. Get your tank on, Carlson, and start handing up those golf balls!"

Carlson didn't budge. "They could be underwater. A big gator can stay underwater for hours at a time. Even I know that. I'm not going in there with any big gators."

Would there be no end to his incessant sniveling? "Okay, okay," I said, "I'll prove it's safe." Years ago, in some forgotten swamp, I had learned how to call gators to the surface of a lake. I now cupped my hands to my mouth and made a low, guttural sound: *ye-UNK UNK, UNK ye-UNK,* then shined the light again.

"Mother of God!" Carlson whispered. "Look at all the eyes!"

It was true. The lake had lit up like a Christmas tree: all the lights wide set and ruby red.

"Maybe they're frogs," Stout said helpfully. "Really big ones."

No, they were gators. Frogs could not have survived in this lake.

"I almost went in there!" Carlson said, sounding near tears. "I could have been eaten!"

There was no reasoning with the man, so we spent the next hour checking the other lakes, lugging our gear along. The most likely lake we found was on the fourteenth fairway: a small water hazard without a tree fringe, and it couldn't have had more than a half dozen small gators cruising around in it. To demonstrate how safe it was, I took my shoes off and waded in up to my knees. But what little spirit Carlson possessed had been broken, and he demanded that we take him and his dry suit home.

"I guess that's the end of it," Stout said to me on the long hike back to the car.

I nudged closer to him so that only he could hear. "Not for us it isn't," I whispered. "When I got in that pond, do you know what I was walking on?" From my pocket I took a handful of golf balls and swept the flashlight across them: Titleist Golden Bears, DTs, MaxFlies, and Dunlops, all pearl white and glistening. "I was ankle-deep in these things. The bottom was covered."

Stout said, "Just for our own self-respect, we need to come back."
"Yeah," I said. "And think of all the money."

Good research is a key element in any successful treasure-hunting venture, and I spent the next few days hard at work. I contacted the Divers Alert Network (DAN) at Duke University Medical Center, which not only provides a twenty-four-hour diving emergency hot line, but also collects data relating to diving injuries and deaths. According to a spokesman there, it was not uncommon for divers to die while salvaging golf balls, and Joel Dovenbarger, director of medical services, Faxed me some accounts that contained interesting details. In my judgment, a high percentage of the fatalities occurred because divers got greedy and overloaded their bags—some were found tied to bags containing from three hundred to five hundred balls. There were no accounts of divers dying from exposure to polluted golf course water, and only one account of a diver being attacked by an alligator. All good news.

Stout and I decided that, before attempting Beach View again, we needed a trial run on a more benign course. We chose Alden Pines, located on Pine Island, only about twenty-five miles from my Fort Myers home. Alden Pines is one of the area's prettiest courses and, because of its narrow fairways, also one of the toughest—in other words, a lot of lost balls. Alden Pines had a couple of more things to recommend it. Because it was built on a bay, its lakes were flushed regularly by the tide, which meant clean water. But more importantly, locals said there was only one really big gator on the whole course—a twelve-footer known affectionately as Martha.

We marched at dusk, an hour after a lightning storm had cleared the fairways. At each lake, I stopped and *ye-UNK UNK UNK*ed, but saw no sign of any gators.

As I told Stout, "It's possible that Martha swam across the bay to Beach View and was eaten."

We found a likely looking lake and went into the water. We didn't have dry suits, but I had invested in an expensive full face mask for reasons that had only a little bit to do with pollution. Although few know about it, there is a diabolical little amoeba found in the silt of some of Florida's freshwater lakes that can swim up a person's mouth or nose, lodge in the brain, and render a person as dumb or dead as a bucket—amoebic meningoencephalitis, the malady is called. To be attacked by an amoeba while dodging alligators is precisely the kind of irony that God seems to relish, and I wasn't going to give Him an opening.

Even though we had seen no gators, it was eerie feeling my way along on the bottom of that lake. But it was also fun. Golf balls appeared luminescent through the gloom, diamond bright and as prolific as toadstools. Every few feet, I would pause to deposit three or four balls into my net dive sack. After less than an hour, Stout and I figured we had about three hundred.

"And these lakes are salvaged regularly," Stout said. "Can you imagine what Beach View must be like?"

With our enthusiasm at full flame, I decided there was no sense in waiting to find out. After depositing about a third of the balls, the country club's share, at the door of the Alden Pines clubhouse (piracy's fine, but I'm no thief) we headed for Beach View where Stout and I flipped to see who would go in the water first.

I lost.

What then transpired is unpleasant to relate for, frankly, I'm not proud of my behavior that night. I am used to pressure-charged situations. Danger, after all, is my business. Even so, swimming around in midnight water with a bunch of giant reptiles would pucker anyone's mettle. Memories of that night return in unwelcome flashes; small incidents that do not reflect the coolheadedness for which I am so well known. At the lake on the fourteenth fairway, I turned to Stout and presented him with a handgun, my 9-mm Sig Sauer semiauto, which I normally only carry in situations of war, or when motoring near the Miami airport. "If an alligator attacks," I told him, "don't hesitate to use this." And when Stout replied that he wasn't sure he could hit a half-submerged alligator, I shouted, "Gator? Hit either one of us, and I'll be happy! But don't miss, Stout. I couldn't bear it if you missed." I also remember hearing a strange, high-pitched whimpering sound as I entered the water; a sad, childlike mewing—and was surprised to realize that it was coming from my own lips. That sound echoed in my mask as I submerged and immediately began to shovel golf balls into a sack. I didn't have to feel for the balls. They were everywhere. The bottom was crusted with them, and I scooped them up by the handful. But I couldn't enjoy it. At any moment, I expected to feel the crushing bite of some big gator—perhaps the behemoth that had apparently devoured Martha. It didn't take long to fill the sack. In fact, I probably overfilled it, because it was a struggle to get back to the surface, where the first words out of Stout's mouth were, "Get out! Get out! We've got company!"

If someone tells you that it is impossible to sprint a mile while wearing a tank, mask, and flippers, that person lacks experience. I know because I did it. Only for a true professional are such feats commonplace. I waited at the car for Stout, who arrived out of breath, and who seemed confused when I demanded, "How big was he? How close did he get? I may go back and wing the bastard just on principle!"

Stout said, "How big was who?"

"Who? The gator that was after me, *that's* who."

Stout was shaking his head. "I didn't see any gators. I thought the night watchman was coming. You never gave me a chance to explain. I thought I saw the lights of a golf cart." Stout was searching around the car. "Hey—where's the bag of balls?"

Back on the bottom of the lake, that's where. In an emergency situation, jettisoning seventy pounds of golf balls is a reasonable act.

"Greed," I told Stout later, "is a disease. How many times have I warned you about that?"

Which is why I never get involved with treasure hunters.

The Big Three

I did not come directly to saltwater fly fishing. Few do. It is a last step, not the first. About the third time a right-handed wind buries a 4/0 short shank into one's hinterlands, the sport begins to invite reinspection. It is less a matter of paying dues than it is waiting until the time is right.

For me, fishing had more to do with the cleaning table than with ceremony. It was an interlude to work, then it became work. I hung corpses out to dry; I stacked them in coolers. The economic expedient influences behavior as surely as one's own antecedents—fishing was a means, not an end. What I liked about it was being on the water, but you don't have to have a rod in your hand to be on the water.

For a time, I preferred a mask and a snorkel. Catch the tide right and I could drift among that which, from a boat, was only imagined. Most divers dislike turbid water, but I never fancied myself as a diver. I loved sliding down a mangrove bank, my own hands ghostly in the murk, stilling myself as a big caudal fin materialized a foot from my mask, then breathless as that frail nucleus assumed mass and shape until finally, it was punctuated by a solitary black eye. Spook a fish that close and the contracting of fast-twitch muscle fiber booms like a snare drum.

For many, the fascination of water lies in its potential: the opportunity to converge with elements as basic as a tidal system; the potential to intersect, in some precise way, with dynamics that may be intuited but are never fully understood.

Think about that, and thrashing around with a mask on one's face will come to seem arbitrary at best.

Not so with fly fishing.

In the last two months, I have had several calls from people wanting to learn about fly fishing. That they would contact a journeyman saltwater caster like me marks their desperation as surely as their number illustrates the pastime's newfound vogue. The callers are mostly upwardly mobile professionals who are focused, articulate; they already know some of the questions to ask. Fin-Nor or Scientific Anglers reel? Sage or Loomis rod?

I answer the questions cheerfully, pleased with their enthusiasm; happy to goad that enthusiasm a little by telling them what is going on in my own angling life. Through the window, from my desk, I can see several fly lines I have stretched from fence to house, so that they will be straight and clean when I need them. By the phone are twenty leaders I have tied and coiled. On the desk behind me, in leather cases, are my reels: a beautiful gold Sea Mater, a Fenwick Big Game, and a couple of Scientific Anglers.

"I'm going to southern Mexico, Sian Ka'an," I tell each of them, "to fish for the big three."

Meaning a bonefish, a tarpon, and a permit—three fish of dissimilar appearance but similar habitat.

Not that I insult my callers by explaining this. If they have any regard for saltwater fly fishing, they know that to hit this spooky trifecta in a single day is the sport's pinnacle. If they haven't, then there is no way to explain why a rational person would spend good money, endure microbes and customs clerks so that he might use the willowiest of tackle to try to catch oversize fish, which, if he is lucky enough to land, he will release anyway.

Silly? Yes, so why risk the discussion.

Nor do I describe to them the sketchpad by the phone. On it I have been designing a hook that I want to make; an idea I have been toying with. The hook will not be curved into a question mark like most hooks. Nor will it be forged of steel or bronze. It will be sharp as a hypodermic, bent into two abrupt Vs, and made of wire so that, instead of having to wait to release the fish, the fisherman can effect the release at any time during the fight simply by allowing the hook to bend free.

Release the fish before you land it? Ridiculous!

You bet. No matter how much they've read, my novitiate callers aren't ready for this. You have to ply the trade for years before you can come to terms with one of the sport's most alluring truths: Fishing excuses any absurdity.

The cover of one of my fishing notebooks reads simply *Central America*, which is appropriate since there are a great many entries about travel in Guatemala, Costa Rica, Nicaragua, Belize,

Panama, and Mexico, though only two or three mentions of actually catching a fish.

Here's an example: "I've finally figured out that the Mayan phrase *Yec-te-tan* means 'I do not understand.' It is what the Guatemalan mountain people reply when I press inquiries about a boat that will take me fly fishing. They smile a little as I pantomime the strange casting motion—am I drunk, or just dancing? They inspect the light rod, presumably vexed by comparisons between it and the more practical hand lines used by their own fishermen. What is the purpose of these feathers tied to a hook when I could use a fresh chunk of fish as bait? Why intentionally make fishing difficult? *Yec-te-tan!*"

Indeed, what is the purpose? I might ask myself that now, standing on the dock at Casa Blanca Lodge, Quintana Roo, southern Yucatán; ask it not in a mood of self-flagellation or soul-searching, but ask it in the spirit my own fishing life has created: amused, self-deprecating, aware that anyone who would go to such lengths to achieve so little is, if not already a doofus, certainly headed that way.

Yec-te-tan. And who does?

Well, maybe I understand just a little. In all directions from this dock, the Caribbean vectors away into a turquoise vacuity. Standing at the vortex is one of the purest pleasures I know. The world is heat saturated, luminous. Seabirds, mangroves, sky, wind. Salt water here is motion without essence; find a straight track of sunlight, and your eyes travel to the bottom without any sense of penetration. But it will float a fly line and, viewed from the dock, even small fish cast shadows.

The Big Three

Not that I am chomping at the bit to break out the rods. We have just arrived, newly landed in the little Cessna that brought us ninety miles from Cancún, and I'd like to get the feel of the place first. Normally, I avoid the Americanized fishing lodges that can be found in every Central American country but El Salvador and Nicaragua. Some people travel to fish, but I fish to travel, so time in an enclave of sports who are still a little hung over from the Dallas airport, and who talk endlessly of spinner baits and bass bustin' . . . well, it seems misspent. The purpose is too tightly focused for me. I prefer the open road where I can use my fishing rods as devices of introduction.

Once, traveling through Guatemala, friends and I were stopped by a band of militia who rousted us from our pickup truck, then frisked us at gun point. I stood with my nose to the door until I noticed several of the men puzzling over my fishing gear. That's one of the great things about a fly rod—almost everyone suspects what it is, but almost no one knows for sure. In short order, I was demonstrating the double haul while the soldiers argued about which local river I should try first. Because any discussion of fishing requires hand gestures, their rifles had been leaned against the trunk where, only moments before, I had stood sweating, scared shitless. As even these men knew, a fisherman is not a worthy object of suspicion. He may be a fool—hell, he's almost certainly a fool—but at least he is benign, and offering assistance to benign fools is more than a good deed; it is an obligation of honor. No matter where you go in the world, natives are proud of the local fishing. Even if they aren't, they'll still drop everything to lie about it.

This trip, though, I have intentionally sought out a place that caters to the growing ranks of saltwater fly fishermen. Built on a low sea promontory of sand and coconut palms, Casa Blanca Lodge is a neat collection of thatched roof cottages that flank a stucco dining hall. The resort has an outpost feel to it, which I like. There is no hint of pretension in its tile floors and lawn of seawrack; no stacks of hunt-and-fish magazines to preoccupy the gut-hook and gaff crowd while they wait for their catch to be iced, measuring success by the blood pounds in their coolers.

"The Caribbean's Finest Light Tackle Fishing" reads the Casa Blanca brochure. Which may be true, though I won't mind if it isn't. I chose Casa Blanca because it is situated in a part of the Yucatán that I have always wanted to see. The lodge is located at the mouth of Ascension Bay, part of the million-acre Sian Ka'an Biosphere, which is a stronghold of indigenous people and has an interesting list of endangered fauna. Here can be found jaguars, tapirs, crocodiles, and more than three hundred species of birds. Unlike most parks, a biosphere reserve allows human habitation as well as the monitored use of natural resources. Which is why Casa Blanca operates with the blessings of the Mexican government, and why more than eight hundred Maya still live and farm and fish near the fallen temples of their forebears.

Standing beside me, my twelve-year-old son, Lee, says, "I'm going to get my mask and snorkel, maybe swim out to the reef." He has already carried his bags to the room, though mine are still on the dock. He hesitates. "Unless you two want some company."

Meaning me and my friend Jeffrey. Jeffrey was one of the top flats guides in the Florida Keys before skin cancer packed him off to saner venues, and he has come along to take photographs and offer advice, plus do a little fishing himself. He already has his gear together, standing in water up to his knees, his right arm lifting, then drifting as the fly rod arcs in synch, each false cast jettisoning deliberate increments of working line.

To Lee, I say, "Good caster, huh?"

"Jeff? Yeah." He watches as Jeffrey's line mimics riverlike oscillations, surging through the looping switchbacks, then taut in a haze of spray. Against a mangrove backdrop the line is singularized, set apart—a lemon-bright filament that animates elements of flight. Lee says, "Nice." Then: "If I see a permit or a tarpon, I'll let you know." His shirt is off, and he's already holding his mask. He waits a moment before adding, "While I'm swimming, I mean."

"Um . . . you see one, just give a holler. I'll get my mask and come right in."

His expression reminds me of something. "I meant so you could get your rod and try to catch it." A picture of the Guatemalan mountain people pops into my mind; that bemused smile.

"Ah, my rod—right. That's just what I'll do. But maybe watch Jeff cast for a while first."

Lee is walking toward the beach—on any journey to the Caribbean, penetrating the water's surface is the final leg of the trip. "Real pretty," he says, still watching Jeffrey.

Our fishing guide, Mario Torres Bolio, is coffee-skinned and wide bodied, and he possesses a certainty of focus that I, happily, lack. Even so, I empathize with him. I empathize with him because for thirteen years I was a guide, a full-time floating businessman who, by taking the objectives of my trade seriously, made a decent living as a fishing pro—a curious occupational turn for a guy who never much liked to fish.

Here's how it happened: In 1974 I got my Coast Guard captain's license and began to canvas marinas near my southwest Florida home, asking if there was work for my boat and me. On Sanibel Island, at Tarpon Bay Marina, the owner, whose name was Mack, said, "We could use another fishing guide; our two slot just opened. The guy blew three power heads in the last six months and decided to go into the lawn-care business."

A generous offer, but I wasn't a fishing guide. "I thought maybe I could hire out to people who wanted to see the back-country. Like birdwatchers. Or do history tours."

As I would learn, Mack's way of dealing with the idiotic was to act as if he took it very seriously. "Ah, history tours. That should pull in some business."

The next morning, six o'clock, the phone rang. It was Mack. "Get your butt out here. You've got four people to fish for snook."

And that's the way it went for more than a decade. The worst year was the first because, though I had grown up fishing, I was a disastrously bad guide. The test is this: If, in the space of four to six hours, you can teach complete strangers how to cast, set the hook, and play a fish, and then find feeding fish on bad tides, in the wind, and if, finally, you can position the boat so these novice casters can reach them with the proper bait, then you are a competent guide.

I wasn't, and I knew it.

To my credit, I believe, I didn't justify my own shortcomings the way most bad guides do. I didn't hang around the dock, grousing about the incompetents I had just suffered; didn't gripe about all the jerks I had to deal with—the people I took out were almost always nice, a truth that didn't vary much over the years. No, the problem was me, and more than once I dropped clients at the dock, only to sneak around the back side of the marina office to refund their money. It was humiliating. I endured it for about six months, then decided I'd either buckle down and learn the trade, or get the hell out.

After that, I had no free days. When I wasn't chartering, I was on the water trying to learn what I should have known in the first place. Did fish always pile on eddy lines, or were they disseminated by tide or instinct or moon stage or God knows what else to the turtle grass flats on the flood? During cold snaps, did fish seek deeper water, or would they move to the shallows so to warm themselves with sunlight? The next twelve months, I had slightly more than a hundred charters, but I spent three hundred days on the boat. I learned knots, I studied charts. If a fisherman, expert or not, had advice to give, I listened—a habit I still practice, the thinking behind it being that you can't learn anything with your mouth open.

This was bait fishing, not fly fishing, but I still learned a couple of things that apply to both disciplines: (1) A fisherman's ego shrinks in proportion to the actual amount of time he or she has spent in the wind, ducking hooks, being made to appear foolish by the unfathomable behavior of fish—something, in time, you will no longer pretend to understand. (2) The habits of fish may be mysterious, but fishing is not. Effective fishing is little more than attention to detail, one bit of knowledge linked to another. (3) Serious fishing is seriously hard work.

By my third season, I judged myself a competent guide and, by my fourth, I probably actually was. I was doing three hundred trips a year and, while I still didn't much like to fish, I took a sort of feverish pleasure in doing it well. Depending on the species sought, and varying with the month, I had my routine broken down into a series of robotic moves employed to produce a maximum amount of fish in the least amount of time. Then it was back to the dock to rebait and re-ice for the next trip.

I had my lines down, too. If someone felt bad about the backlash they'd caused or the fish they'd missed: "If that's the worst thing you do in your life, you're in good shape." On how many pounds of fillets they could expect to ship home: "Go to a fish market, you'll save money."

Remarks used to comfort, deflect, and amuse the steady flow of Midwesterners, Northeasterners, and other outlanders who were my clients; a generally pleasant bunch who ranged from beer-pounding conventioneers, to Ma and Pa on a dream vacation, to the famous or powerfully rich, most of whom, once isolated on a small boat in strange waters, proved to be just people, nothing less; people trying to get by in life and maybe have a little fun along the way.

By my fourth season, I began to think in terms of building a reputation. Fishing guides think like that—as if specialization is a way to make one's mark, even in a field where all accomplishment is as ephemeral as a scaled creature's heartbeat. I decided I wanted to be known as a light-tackle tarpon specialist. On my coast, there are no bonefish; permit were an esoteric occasional more appropriately associated with the Florida Keys and flats pioneers such as Captain Jimmy Albright, Stu Apte, and Chico

Fernandez. Where I worked, tarpon were the glamour species. Plus, I liked the way these giant herringlike animals looked and moved. Each spring, for reasons no researcher yet understands, tarpon would appear in the littoral: wild pods of broaching fish, six feet long, chromium bright, and mindless as beams of light. It was a fish that, in its driven behavior and prehistoric physiology, implied some deeper design. What, no one knew. You could hook them, touch them, gaff them, hang them, stuff them, visit upon them any outrage, even dissect them, but that part of their life, the design and movement of it, was still private, beyond reach or understanding. I don't know why I found that so compelling, but I did. I do.

I undertook to learn what there was to know of tarpon. Coincidentally, at about the same time, a man showed up at the docks and asked in the shiest and most apologetic way if he could hire me to take him fly fishing. I found it touching. At that time, people didn't fly fish Florida's southwest coast. It was too deep, too murky, too shallow, always too something; reasons varied. After all, saltwater fly fishing was still in its fledgling days, gathering slow, slow momentum down on the Keys.

"We'll take some bait, just in case," I told him.

"There's no need for that. I won't use it."

"You probably won't catch anything," I said, making sure he knew in advance just exactly who was off the hook.

"I don't care."

Well, I had heard that before, but I took him, anyway.

It was pretty watching him cast. That's one detail I remember about that trip. The casting motion was lean and metronomic, but in a way that gave the impression of improvisation. It was a thing that shared its grace. Equally memorable was that the guy caught fish—dazzling, considering that he was making all the concessions, giving each of those small sea trout and redfish fair opportunity to go about their own lives. Unlike using bait in its death throes, or plastic lures punched from a mold and stamped with eyes, there seemed something bedrock honest about a small streamer fly made of game hair.

Most memorable of all was this: Blind casting the grass flats, a tarpon ate the guy's fly, savaged the adjacent water for a microsecond, vaulted the boat, vaulted it again, popped the leader, then greyhounded off, leaving us both shivering like wet dogs, goofy with shock.

"*Jesus Lord.*"

"Did you see that?"

"Holy shit!"

"Came out of no where and *ate.*"

"Did you see that?!"

"*That's what I'm saying!*"

So much for the accepted fishing wisdom of a region.

I'd like to pretend that I was an instant convert to fly fishing: that, on that day, I began the journey to what is, in this instance, Casa Blanca Lodge, southern Yucatán, meaning the proving ground of one's own fieldcraft—if such a place can exist.

Not so. I found fly fishing intimidating. All that discourse about fly fishing being an "art," the unfamiliar terminology; plus there was an elitist feel to it that was as foreign to me as Orvis tweeds and jodhpurs.

Over the next year, I would piece together the reality: Fly fishing, at best, is a craft, not an art; memorizing a dozen new words solves most of the nomenclature problems; and what's wrong with Orvis tweeds? Also, I would learn how to cast—a skill I acquired on my own, practicing when and where no one could see. Privately.

In the meantime, though, I stuck with matters at hand. Each spring morning, I was in my boat, bait swarming beneath the aerator spray, leaders tied, hooks sharpened, beginning to fume if my clients were even a little bit late, my patience draining with the tide. It didn't matter what excuses or disclaimers they brought aboard with them. They could wax on and on about the beauty of the day, hint they wouldn't mind substituting a picnic for the fishing, promise they didn't give a damn if we wet a line or not, and it was all just more catalyst in an ever-hardening resolve.

I knew what they wanted, even if they did not.

Which is why I empathize with Mario Bolio, our guide. He met us at the Cessna yesterday afternoon and, as we walked from the packed-sand landing strip, he said he was excited about helping me try to take the big three on a fly, but that it had rained hard for the last five days.

"The fishing—maybe not so good now."

That was fine with me. "I don't care if we catch anything or not."

I recognized the dubious look he gave me. How many times had I given it myself?

"No, I mean it. It is of no importance."

His expression didn't change.

"Honest!"

We talked along, me speaking in poor Spanish, him answering in slightly better English—a thing that is humorous in itself but is, in my experience, a common way of conversing in Central America.

"¿En la mañana? ¿Cuando . . . pescado . . . I mean, pescamos?"

"What time to fish you mean?"

"Sí. Hora. ¿A qué hora?"

"Today, we fish now. Palometta on fly, very difficult. Every day, all the time, we must fish."

"Palometta?"

"You call 'permit.'"

"Oh, *permit.*"

Yes, a permit would undoubtedly be the hardest of the three species to take on a fly. There are competent anglers who have fished permit for years, cast crab flies at thousands, and have never had a single taker. But I was still shaking from the plane ride. I wanted to get a beer and roam around a little. Which is what I did—looking down at the dock occasionally, to see Lee swimming, Jeffrey casting, and Mario futzing with his boat, probably fuming a little, too.

This morning, though, Mario is in charge, the three of us positioned just the way he wants in his fifteen-foot tri-hull with its thirty-horse Yamaha Enduro engine. Our fly rods are belted port and starboard, the water jug is full, Jeffrey has his cameras plus a battery of flies, Lee has his mask and snorkel ("In case we don't have to fish all the time") and I am equipped with the accoutrement of a modern sport: a pair of polarized sunglasses, shirt by Cabellás, shorts by Patagonia, shoes by Omega—the overall effect being one of some meat hanger who probably roughed up the aisle clerks before robbing Abercrombie & Fitch. Truth is, I feel a little overwhelmed by all the equipage. Tomorrow, I have already decided, I go back to the way I normally fish: T-shirt, barefooted, with a pretty scarf I bought in Cuba to keep off the sun.

Mario steers us through a series of saltwater creeks, and I position myself sufficiently outboard to watch the bottom blur by: marl plateaus eroding toward sand basins that are copper streaked, startlingly bright beyond the shade of mangroves. Then shoals of turtle grass, the bowed blades defining the direction of tide in the same way wheat fields illustrate wind. A pink coral head jumps past, and fish flush: small snappers, barracuda, a few bonefish.

I glance at Mario. He has turned inward, running the boat by rote, so I know we are nowhere close to the bottom we will fish. I think of it in those terms: What bottom and where? For, if one plies the trade long enough, one ceases to think of water as water, but more specifically as a choral element that is, because it is affected by wind, and because it flows in lunar patterns, one more factor to be considered in regard to the terrain one covets. On the Great Lakes, the walleye-heads might fish at forty feet or sixty feet, hunting the thermoclines. In the Atlantic, bill fishermen might troll the fifty-fathom line. But on the flats, you fish banks and rips and mesas; contours of land sculpted by current and nearer in appearance to the sand rifts of a desert. On the flats, three feet of water is considered extreme.

We exit out into Laguna Pájaros, a bay that is an expanding region of green. The water is light-saturated, a radiant gel that diffuses the neat boundaries of sea and space, creating pale demarcations of color. Everything is luminous, but nothing is defined. At one moment, we seem to be riding through a green concavity; the next moment, careening down the skin of a massive blue sphere. Then Mario points to an isolated charcoal stroke on the horizon: an island. "We fish there."

Me: "¿Qué pescados . . . pescamos allí?"

Mario: "What kind fish? *Macavi*. Bonefish." He smiles, awakening to the hunt.

I smile back because I like Mario. On the boat, he's all business, but ashore he softens a bit and doesn't mind conversation. He grew up speaking Mayan to his mother, and I think he appreciates it when I try the few Mayan words I know. When our boat first panicked a cormorant to flight, I nudged him and said, "Cheech."

Surprised, Mario chuckled. "Bird, yes. A bird." Then he corrected me: "ChEECH."

Lee is *impal*, my son. I am *tata*, Lee's father. *Xtabay* is a kind of spirit; a forest ghost with silky hair like a woman, but the feet of a turkey. And that's about all the Mayan I know, except for *yec-te-tan*, about which Mario has already told me an ironic story. When the conquistadors arrived, he said, they asked the Maya, in Spanish, the name of their land. Naturally, the Maya did not understand, and said so.

On maps, *yec-te-tan* became Yucatán.

As the boat carries us across the bay, shadows of cumulus clouds drift before us, gathering speed. The bellies of the clouds are jade tinted, holding light or holding water—I don't know which. Mario no longer steers by rote; his head pivots back and forth, measuring the water plain.

Though they were not a species available to me as a guide, and though I have caught only a few off a fly, I still have a particular fondness for bonefish. The first bonefish I ever took was off Cay Caulker, Belize, thanks to a local who steered me by the shoulder to a muddy little water pocket, and who then pointed, saying, "Dah boneyfish, deh live dere, mon."

He meant they lived on the flats?

"No, mon—the boneyfish, deh live dere." He pointed to the mud pocket again; it covered an area no bigger than a refrigerator.

Yes, bonefish hunted close to shore. I already knew that.

"I tell you, mon, dat where deh be living! Right there!" Finger at the mud pocket again.

My brother, who had already waded out, looked at me and shrugged. I shrugged back, and made a cast into the mud pocket, just to please the local. An instant later, a fish was on the fly, taking line—and it ran right between the legs of my brother, who, in a garble of surprise, began to wail, "Ooh-ooh-ooh—WHOA!" as he tried, without dignity, to dismount my line.

Whenever I see a bonefish now, I grin. I hook one, I begin to chuckle.

I chuckle a lot this afternoon. At Cedro Key, where nesting cormorants and frigates burp and growl like lions, I take my first bone, aware that Mario is judging my casting ability, gauging just what his chances are of connecting me with the big three. His reaction to a decent cast is, "Good! Now streep! Streep!" His reaction to a cast that spooks fish is a whispered, "*Sheesh.*"

I hear both.

A bonefish is a strange-looking creature with a head like an Amazon bird and a tail that seems oversize for its body, unless one has experienced the speed of it, meteoriting across the shallows, in which case the tail, at least, makes perfect sense. When I bring the first bonefish to the boat, I lift the weight of it—there is a wonderful density to even a small bonefish—and I hear Jeffrey say, "One down and two to go."

Four hours later, though, it is still one down and two to go. At Punta Hualatoc, not far from the landing strip, Mario puts me on permit, the size of which actually made my knees shake. Crouched beside me, his cameras ready, Jeffrey would call, "See the spike? See the spike?" meaning the cobalt point of tail, or the periscoping spine of the fish's second dorsal fin. Each permit I saw traveled with deliberation, absolutely purposeful in its movement, yet displacing great volumes of water as it foraged, warping the water surface with its bulk.

"Jesus, they're all so damn big."

"There's the spike again—cast!"

I casted to dozens of them, thinking, perversely, that, if one hit, my light rod and I were in for serious trouble. Occasionally, I could see the whole fish through the water, its body appearing as a series of crescent angles joined by a pearlescent skin, pale as moonlight. Seeing them made my throat go dry. They were as intimidating as *samurai*, with their scimitar dorsals and scythian tails, and it was shameful how relieved I was when they showed no interest in my fly. None did. I would cast in a way so as to lead them, as a quarterback might lead a receiver. I would wall the fly in, ever closer, like artillery. Balls to the wall, I would throw right at them, hoping to shock them into a strike—but, instead, shocked only Mario, who had poled his butt off to get me close enough just to have me spook them.

Sheesh!

But a permit that will eat a fly is an anomaly. Better casters than I had spent obsessive, bewildered years proving just that. And if I didn't believe it before, I certainly believed it after a few tight-sphincter hours fishing Punta Hualatoc.

"Ah, screw it! These fish would eat a tomato before they'd eat a fly."

Jeffrey: "We could try another flat."

"No, let's can it. Give Mario a break and just have fun. Hey, Mario—¡Por favor, vamos pescar sabalo? No tienen hambre."

"You are not hungry?"

"No, the permit, el palometta, they aren't hambre—"

"Tarpon, you fish? Go now?"

"Sure. You bet. Es no importante."

Another day, we travel to a deep backcountry area called Santa Rosa, pulling the skiff through mangrove tunnels hand over hand, then exiting into lakes the color of smokey crystal. Once, after miles of nothingness, we rounded a bend to find the stone ruins of a Mayan temple, wild orchids and dildo cactus growing from the blocks of coquina rock, and iguanas baking themselves in the heat and silence. But no tarpon—Mario said all the rain had flushed them.

Which left bonefish; hundreds of bonefish, thousands of bonefish. Miss your forecast, and they'd take on the backcast. Standing in knee-deep water, intent on the tidal guttering and sand whorls which concentrated my attention as surely as they funneled fish, I said to Lee, "You want to catch another?"

"No. It's kind of fun watching."

"You'd have rather spent more time exploring that temple, huh?"

"Yeah, I'll go back there anytime."

"Your little brother, he'd rather fish."

"For hours. I don't know how he does it."

"Miss him?"

"Um, I don't know."

"I miss him, too."

Later, in our room, as Lee began to doze, I would touch my hand to his leg, a whorled shape beneath the bed covers, and whisper, "I'll tell you a secret."

He stirred. "You'd have rather spent more time exploring the temple, too?"

I was going to tell him that, when I was his age, I didn't like to fish, either. Instead, I said, "You got it."

Two A.M. and I am wondering: *Why is that true—I never liked to fish?*

My earliest memories are of fishing; it was something I learned as naturally as Colorado children probably learned skiing. For my mother, who had been obsessed and overwhelmed with work since childhood in a Carolina mill town, fishing was her only hobby. The same with my many uncles.

With her, it was out digging night crawlers and cutting bamboo poles to size. With my uncles, it was collecting catawba caterpillars, or fishing bass lures on spinning rods.

Even now, if I see a worm, I picture it curved into the shape of a hook.

Around the dinner table, my Southern family included—still includes—the funniest people I have ever known. Swirling their iced tea in Mason jars, they'd get me laughing until I cried. The quiet was sheered up with talk about bream and sunfish (robin, we called them) and where and for what we might fish next.

What I remember best were the porcupine quills my mother favored as bobbers. At the most delicate touch of the tiniest fish, a porcupine quill will vanish beneath water; an implosion as precise as the loop of a well-thrown fly line.

In a tackle shop, my eyes still linger on them, taking pleasure.

For a period, when I was old enough to fish on my own, I did a lot of it. I would make dough balls of cotton and bread, and catch catfish in the small town pond. There was a boy who got in the habit of joining me, a classmate named Perry Grey—his real name. Perry was one of those unfortunate children who, because he was tiny and not very clean, became the butt of school jokes; a pariah who could only be touched at a price.

Cooties! He's got cooties!

Once, Perry insisted that I come home with him to see the flying squirrel he had caught. His house was no smaller than my own, but I remember that it was very dark inside, and that it stank of something—soured whiskey and urine? Not knowing any better, I would, for years, associate that odor with flying squirrels.

Each time I carried a pole to the pond, Perry would materialize like a shadow. Which was okay; he loved to fish, and he was a nice kid, though I hated it when he began to trail me on the playground. But one afternoon, when some classmates chanced upon us at the pond, I rallied the cruelty to do what I had been unable to do before: told Perry I didn't want him tagging after me any more. "Get out of here, I didn't invite you— I mean it."

Some days later, not more than a week, my mother was reading the paper, and I heard her say, "That poor, poor child." Then she went to show the piece to my father, and I heard her say, "He got the rope up, but he couldn't reach it, even from a chair, so he had to stand in his mother's high heels."

As I said, Perry Grey was a tiny boy.

It was at about this time that fishing began to create wide spaces of silence that I felt could have been better used. I fancied that it began to interfere with baseball.

My mother, though, kept right on working and fishing, fishing and working until something had to give, and it finally did. My cousin Kerney (whom we call Chucky, for reasons I still don't understand) is now minister at the Church of God in Hamlet, North Carolina, and he spoke at her funeral. He looked down at me from the pulpit, grinned, winked, and said, "I bet Georgia taught most everybody in this church how to fish. Why, her boy Randy's become famous for it. Can't you just see her now, up there in heaven, with a chaw of tobacco, sayin' 'Bite fish! Dang you, bite!' Yes sir, I bet that's what Georgia's doin' right now."

The effect of which was about the same as being with them all at the dinner table.

Jeffrey took me aside tonight and asked, "You ever think much about what it is we actually do?"

"Huh?"

"As guides. Our relationship to fish? I'm finding it harder and harder to justify hooking them, causing them to swim around at top speed, under stress, just for my own pleasure or profit."

This is what Jeffrey said, or something like it—I was drinking beer, not taking notes.

I told him, "As a matter of fact, I have." Then, with a piece of shark wire, I made the hook I had designed; the hook that would bend free at any chosen moment, always dependent upon the angler's mood; his personal gauging of just how long he felt good about being connected to a fish. A big tarpon, which, after an hour, comes up belching like a blown horse, could, instead, be freed after fifteen minutes. A bonefish could be sent on its way after five.

At least, that's what the hook was supposed to do.

Jeffrey considered the tiny thing with a professional eye; touched the point. "It needs to be a lot sharper."

"Of course. But you see how it works?"

"You know—it might. It might work at that. Let's make a couple, and I'll put them in the vise. Little shrimp ties for bones."

"I've already got a name for it," I said. I didn't, but I was suddenly feeling overly sensitive. I mean, we were discussing the momentary discomfort of creatures that were, after all, just fish. And it wasn't as if we hurt them, then humiliated them back at the docks by hanging them on display. "If it works," I said, "I'll call it the Premature Emancipation Hook." Which, I felt, gave the whole business a nice masculine flavor, while also paying tribute to the absurdity of such a thing.

"We can try it tomorrow," Jeffrey said. "Can you imagine the look on Mario's face? We'll have one mad Mayan on our hands."

I imagined the poor guy thinking, *Yec-te-tan*.

Actually, we tried the Premature Emancipation Hook on our last day at Casa Blanca. More accurately, Jeffrey tried it. Not me. Fishing affords many kinds of intersecting; provides continuity, one disparate step to another, with a lone bright filament that links many decisions with God's own number of lives. My decision was to spend the day with Lee, swimming and walking the beach.

Jeffrey said that the hook worked okay, and our guide wasn't mad a bit.

Like me, Mario was probably still feeling a little woozy from the morning before when, boom-boom-boom-boom, just like that, I landed a mutton snapper, a bonefish, a tiny tarpon, and a permit—the saltwater trinity, plus one, all on fly.

Ice Angler Shoot-Out

Granted, this is anecdotal data, but it is my experience that airport X-ray machines disturb, alter, or somehow variegate the fish-catching properties of terrestrial annelids, family Lumbricidae, those slimy little crawlers known commonly as earthworms. To me, this was both a surprise and a disappointment. Prior to competing in the Midwest Ice Angler's Championship at Waconia, Minnesota, I had spent weeks in careful preparation . . . no easy task because my home state is not on the auger-and-sauger tour; ice fishing has yet to enjoy a South Florida vogue. I visited the library. I made telephone calls. The Touch-Tone triplex, area code 612, became the theme prelude to exhaustive, fishy monologues. I learned that walleye, crappie, bass, sauger, and northern pike were the available quarry, and that fathead minnows, suckers, and maggots were the baits of choice.

To a veteran saltwater guide and fly fisherman such as myself, this was all the rankest kind of talk.

"Why not use earthworms?" I asked.

"'Cause they shatter like glass after you dig 'em out of three feet of snow," a Minnesotan explained. "Got to warm 'em in your mouth just to get a heartbeat. That's what the folks from Iowa tell me, anyway." Minnesotans—gee, how they love to joke.

That conversation focused my whole approach to the Midwest Ice Angler's Championship. It was true that officials estimated the MIAC shoot-out would attract more than four thousand of the region's most accomplished ice fishermen to Waconia. It was also true that I had no ice-fishing experience. But on the way to the airport, when my teammate, Johnson, asked how I thought we would do, I answered without hesitation: "I think we'll win," I told him. "Even if God loses track of our itinerary, we'll place in the top ten."

Johnson lacked my confidence. "You've never caught a walleye in your life," he said. "Not one. Admit it."

"Admit it? Hell, I'm proud of it." I was, too. In thirteen years as a guide, I had dealt with hundreds of vacationing Midwesterners— nice people, but even the self-proclaimed experts cast like nerve gas victims. Conversationally, their opening gambit did not vary: "You ever hear of a walleye? Best eating fish in the world. We catch 'em by the hundreds."

As I told Johnson, "To run afoul of those Bohunks, the walleye has to be one of the stupidest fish on Earth. Just smart enough to breed and sizzle."

For some reason, Johnson took umbrage at this. "Minnesotans aren't Bohunks," he interrupted. "Minnesotans are Gophers.

People from Wisconsin are Bohunks. Or . . . Badgers? No, wait—people from Wisconsin are *Cheeseheads*. But we are definitely Gophers." Which reminded me that Johnson, though he had spent the last ten years playing baseball in Florida, was the grandson of immigrant Norwegians and was, himself, a native Minnesotan.

Chastened but confused, I amended: "Sorry. The stupidest *Gophers* on Earth."

Johnson grinned. "That's better. Now you're learning!" Having volunteered as my guide and interpreter for this trip, the man took his teaching duties seriously.

But he was missing the point. At the airport, I took a plastic container from my carry-on and popped the lid. Inside were six dozen fat night crawlers, all handpicked for their sluggish come-and-eat-me qualities. Those on the surface retracted listlessly into the mulch, reacting to the neon light. "This is why we're going to win the Midwest Ice Anglers Championship," I explained to Johnson. "Lake Waconia has been under the ice for how long? Since November? Those fish haven't seen anything but fathead minnows and maggots for three months. They're starving for a menu change. Drop these night crawlers through the ice, and we will have a genuine feeding frenzy on our hands." I returned the container to my briefcase and zipped the briefcase shut. "We're going to win this contest, Lefty." (Like all southpaw pitchers, Johnson liked to be called "Lefty.") "We'll be the only ones there using night crawlers for bait. Trust me. I know about fish. Don't forget: I'm a professional, and we're dealing with amateurs."

After our carry-ons had passed through the X-ray chute and we were waiting to board, Johnson said to me, "I wouldn't mind looking at those worms again. Maybe hold one? All I saw was dirt."

I handed him the plastic container and watched him peek under the lid. He said, "Um-m-m . . . those walleyes are lucky!" But then his expression changed, and he yanked his hand away as if he had just touched something hot. "Hey!" he said. "Ouch!" Johnson smacked the lid, sealing it. His face described shock and outrage. "Those little bastards tried to bite me!"

A ridiculous charge. Obviously, the pressure of tournament fishing was already affecting the big left-hander, and I grabbed the container before he had a chance to hurl it across the terminal. "Lefty," I said soothingly, "worms don't bite. They were trying to hide. Night crawlers are very shy"—I had opened the carton to show him—"and nonaggressive little slugs that react to light. See, if you try to touch them they . . . they . . . whoa! Jesus!" Suddenly and inexplicably, the worms were snapping at my wrists and trying to barber-pole up my fingers. "Gad!"

It took some time, but I managed to wrestle the lid shut.

"I don't think they're going to let those worms into Minnesota," Johnson said, backing away. "They're *mean*."

It was true. In the span of a few seconds, some terrible force had transformed my lymphatic night crawlers into six dozen writhing devil worms, active as pit vipers.

I was still struggling to hold the lid down. "It must have been the X-ray machine," I said, remaining calm. "It's thrown their metabolism completely out of whack. I need some tape. Fast! We need to secure this container before we get on that plane."

It was then I learned something about Minnesotans: They never go anywhere without duct tape or a muffler. (As Johnson would later explain, "If duct tape won't fix it, you still got the option of strangling it.")

I got the container sealed, then spent the next fifteen minutes reassuring Johnson that if we suffered a midflight worm spill, I would die fighting before I allowed our uranium-zapped night crawlers to advance to the first class bulkhead, never mind about the cockpit and crew beyond.

We landed at Minneapolis–St. Paul International in the January gloom of six P.M.: silos and black trees then skyscrapers and lights on a dusk-swollen snow prairie. The night before, I had been hitting ground balls at Little League practice. Now, an electronic bank sign near the airport read −15°; a temperature change of approximately ninety degrees.

"That's not even counting the windchill factor," Johnson said cheerfully as we drove toward his boyhood home, the pretty little farming community of Janesville, an hour and a half southwest of Minneapolis.

This was something else I would learn about Minnesotans: Windchill factor is a beloved safe harbor of exaggeration, perhaps because these staunch, upright people allow themselves no other acceptable social outlet for lying. If the temperature column in the *Minnesota Star-Tribune* read: "Damn cold: Pick your own numbers," the citizenry could not have taken more perverse pride in their own chilly bravado, and I'm sure that somewhere in Minnesota at least one gravestone reads: "One below—not counting windchill."

But we were in a car, the heater roaring like a pig iron furnace. Still, Johnson took time to muse, "With the windchill factor, it's

probably forty, maybe a hundred degrees below freezing outside."
Then he added innocently, "You put those worms in the trunk
like I told you?"

No. They were still in my briefcase. Snug and toasty on the
backseat, hopefully filled with their own augmented fire.

It was our plan to spend a couple of days in Janesville, ready-
ing our equipment and gathering ice fishing intelligence before
journeying fifty miles north to Waconia for the championship
fish-off on Saturday. My reasoning was simple: If the Waconia
touts learned of my presence, my reputation, or my worms, our
chances of getting odds on ourselves in a fat Calcutta were nil.
(As it turned out, there was no gambling at the MIAC—something I found hard to believe until I had experienced the horrible fishing.) As for Johnson, he was only too happy to spend a
few days revisiting his boyhood haunts. He took me to the baseball diamond where he had begun his career ("Pitcher's mound's
around here someplace," he said, stomping through the drifts.
"Check that snowbank and I bet you'll find the backstop"), and,
at night, we held down stools at the 3's Company Bar or the
Legion Hall where Johnson's old teammates (from a graduating
class of only forty-six) greeted his return with a minimum of
emotion but a whole bunch of free Grain Belt beer. I liked
Janesville with its elms and oaks and grange meetings. The shoveled sidewalks and smoking chimneys added warmth and order to
the white hush of winter. And I liked the people. They said,
"You don't say!" when enthused and "OOF-dah!" when exasper-
ated. They told spooky stories about the nearby village of
Pemberton where some of the people, they said, were sadly
inbred, and where the local bartender always wore surfing shorts

("Even when it's thirty below—not counting windchill!"), and where a child with more than two fingers was considered potentially gifted.

I also gathered a lot of information about ice fishing, although it was tough to get a consensus of opinion about anything. When I asked about hook size, knots, depth, water temperature, or kindred details, the replies always included careful disclaimers: "I'm not saying this for certain . . ." or, "You'll probably want to check with somebody else, but . . ." Minnesotans, I decided, take pride in their personal accountability so they are damn careful about what it is they are being accountable for. But when I confided to the local fire chief that I was going to use Florida earthworms in the Midwest Ice Anglers Championship, he dropped his guard: "You don't say! Why . . . by golly . . . you just might catch *something.*"

As Johnson said on Friday, as we drove along the ice-bright Minnesota River toward Waconia, "I love this state. The place never changes."

Johnson and I spent Friday night in beautiful little Waconia (pop. 3,700) out on the lake in our own rental fish house. It was a cozy little room on skids, 8' × 10', with a propane stove, bunks covered with shag carpet, and auger holes already drilled for our convenience. Each hole had its own tiny lightbulb that reflected a turquoise disc of lake water, plus we were provided with an iceskimming ladle and maggots. I immediately stowed my gear, baited a hook with a maggot, and dropped the bait down a hole.

"Why don't you use a worm?" Johnson wanted to know. "Afraid to open the lid?"

No. In a hard-crunch fishing tournament, smart players save their best bait for the actual dance. And I wasn't going to waste my earthworms on a meaningless practice session.

"Quiet," I said. "I'm concentrating." I sat touching the line, waiting for the change in tension that would communicate the first tentative interest of the walleyes I pictured swarming down below. I waited. I sat. I sat and waited some more. Then I tried fishing different depths. An hour passed before I tried fishing different holes. Finally, I told Johnson, "This business of using maggots is some fishing entrepreneur's idea of an obscene joke. I can't believe I fell for it!" Then I said, "Hand me the worms— but we're only going to use *one*."

Johnson was already moving. "Now you're talking! Hey . . . where the hell did my gloves go?"

I slashed the tape and opened the carton. While my night crawlers didn't display the same writhing ethos as earlier, they still behaved with a feisty screw-you attitude that is only one of many symptoms associated with uranium poisoning. I pinned a fat one, loaded it on the hook, and dropped it down the chute.

Nothing. Not a breath of activity. I hunkered down to wait while Johnson busied himself with my shortwave radio, tuning in Radio Finland ("I didn't know they spoke English in Finland!") and then by savaging our supplies, trying to prepare dinner: "You want maple syrup on your Spam, right?"

"No!"

I handed him the fishing rod while I tried to rescue our entrée.

Only a few seconds passed before Johnson said, "Hum-m-m. Hoo! I think I just had a bite."

I put down the skillet and touched the line. There was a hint of weight below; it was as if he had snagged a drifting tissue. "That's no fish. Your bait has probably iced up. Check it."

He hauled the line in hand over hand . . . and there was an ice-numbed minnow on his hook. "Crappie!" Johnson exclaimed. "Nice one, too!" The poor thing was about the size of an aspen leaf, though not as animated.

But the worms worked. Here was proof. "Lefty," I said, "practice is over. Let's go talk to our neighbors and see if anyone's interested in a friendly wager."

Although I didn't realize it at the time, I would learn far more about the charm of ice fishing that night than I would learn during the whole next day of tournament fishing. All around us was a strange, random community suspended on the frozen lake; a jumbled geometric haze of portable shelters cluttering the expanse of white. Connecting them was a network of roads plowed by an ice scraper. The squatty little sheds, with their fuming chimneys, illustrated what life in the Arctic might be like.

Johnson and I roamed around talking with fishermen, trading cans of beer and stories. They were nice people. They laughed a lot. Among them were ice fishing tackle reps hawking their products, and they showed us how to stake a "tip-up" rod (a length of fiberglass about three feet long; no reel) and how the spring-loaded flag indicates that a fish has struck. They demonstrated how a gas muscle-auger can punch a hole in two-foot ice in less than a minute, and they debated which brand of snow mobile had torque enough to pull a "fully equipped" fish house.

The men and women of Lake Waconia were very proud of their fish houses and quick to offer tours. Many of the sheds were as smartly appointed as mobile homes, with their televisions, VCRs, stereos, propane stoves, and chemical toilets. These nice people went to great lengths and expense to stay comfortably inside while they were outside on the lake.

As one man told me, "If you think this is something, you ought to get up to Brainerd. They got eight thousand ice shacks on the lake up there! You like to play poker? That's the place. Some ice towns even got their own hookers."

The man wasn't talking about terminal tackle—indeed, catching fish seemed incidental to this whole, strange ceremony.

As the *Minnesota Star-Tribune*'s outdoor columnist, Ron Schara, would later tell me, "Ice fishing isn't so much a sport as it is a social happening. It's a way to get outdoors, have some laughs, and a good excuse for people with common interests to get together. Catching fish doesn't have a lot to do with it."

The next morning and afternoon, at the Midwest Ice Anglers Championship, I would find out why. Statistically speaking, there were no fish.

The day of the tournament was clear and sunny (the temperature zoomed to twenty degrees above zero—not counting windchill) yet only between two and seven fish over six ounces (the minimum weight) were caught, depending upon whom you believe. The results, frankly, are sketchy, and there are some tricky legal matters involved, so I must be delicate. The promoter, who charged thirty-five dollars per adult entrant, said only 1,800 anglers entered. The *Waconia Patriot* estimated 2,800. A man who said he caught the day's second biggest fish, a two-pound northern pike, was challenged by the promoter to take a lie detector test. "He failed miserably," the promoter told me. "We think he brought it [the pike] in in his pants."

There were also dark rumors concerning one or two other fish that were entered. "It's true," the promoter said, "that a small yellow perch that won a prize isn't a species normally found in Lake Waconia, but we didn't challenge it. It's also true that there were suspicions about another fish that was entered, but I'm not going to talk about that."

As Ron Schara told me, "People in the business have, for some time, had an inkling that a group of guys from Wisconsin has been winning or placing too high to be accredited to angling skill. They're a promoter's nightmare."

When I passed that news along to Johnson, he yelled, "Those bastard Cheeseheads!" My X-ray-bonged earthworms didn't attract another bite and in six hours of hard fishing, we caught zero, *nada*, zilch. The worms went into our ice hole fighting like Godzilla, but they came back out a subdued marl blue—which was the same color as my toes after a day of that madness.

Yet, as Johnson pointed out on the plane ride home, "The way I figure it, we tied for a spot in the top ten easy. We didn't catch anything, but no one else did, either."

He cheered me only slightly. I wasn't angry at the Cheeseheads. The day-to-day existence of a man who will pack a pike in his pants is its own punishment. But I was still deeply stung and, frankly, humiliated by the behavior of Waconia's walleyes. Two thousand or more different baits dangling through the ice, all day long, and not one of those bastards had brains enough to take advantage of it.

As I told Johnson, "I just don't have any respect for that fish."

Ironman with Fly

I n decades to come, when the Vail Ironman of Fly Fishing
Championship of the World has acquired the respect it
deserves, when networks are battling over rights to exclusive
coverage, when shoe companies and nutrition behemoths are
baiting competitors with cold cash and long-term endorsement
contracts, it is likely—very likely—that Glenn Lokay, the event's
founder, will cast a dyslexic eye back upon the list of inaugural
contestants, and he will pause long enough to curse and spit my
name.

If the man can remember my name. Nothing against Lokay,
but the degenerate lifestyle of western fly-fishing guides is well
documented; brain cells are the first casualties of their loathsome
excesses. Put these men and women in chest waders, stand them
in a glacial river, and their passion for respectable, productive
lives will dissolve as quickly as their prissiness regarding personal

hygiene. Place them in a bar or in the gutter of any far-flung mountain town—ditto. All they talk about, all they care about, is moving water and wild trout. Paint sniffers are more eclectic dinner companions.

Which is why I was so surprised when, last fall, Lokay telephoned to invite me to his Ironman of Fly Fishing; "The first annual," he called it—a wistful name which not only implied that there would be a second, but also credited Lokay with foresight and organizational skills not often associated with people who have built their lives around animals that spawn.

"I've invited all the top Colorado guides," Lokay told me, "all the best men and women west of the Divide. But we'd also like to get some saltwater fly fishermen involved. A real world championship—see? Naturally, your name is at the top of my list. *Número uno*. What'd they call you in Florida? 'Captain Amazing'?"

As a western guide, Lokay is atypical only in that he owns and operates his own tackle shop, Vail's Gore Creek Fly Fisherman, and he is often emboldened by this patina of respectability. Even so, it was uncharacteristic of him to resort to such noxious flattery; that he had recalled my nickname accurately made it no less offensive.

"Let me guess," I countered. "It's October and Vail has more empty rooms than the Bates Motel. Now you've contrived some absurd competition to rally your business."

"I'm going to ignore that," Lokay replied. "This is a legitimate event. Too many people view fly fishing as a snob sport—I don't blame them. The Ironman is a reply for those of us who still do it for fun. We've only had a week to plan it; I don't know how many will show up, but it's going to be great. Next year, it'll be bigger; people will be begging to compete."

That, at least, would prove to be true.

I listened as Lokay listed the events: distance casting; fly casting one hole of golf; blindfolded knot tying; accuracy casting; a one-fly fish-off; an upriver distance run, through Vail, dressed in underwear only—waders optional.

"Gad!" I said, "you had to be drunk when you thought this thing up."

"Well, sure . . . *legally*. Otherwise, I was fine. Had a nice creative edge. You'll see, this'll be a real test of your abilities. A chance to show the river guides just how good you saltwater casters really are."

More flattery, and utterly transparent: Lokay, aware that I know nothing about trout fishing, clearly saw this as an opportunity to humiliate me and to debase the things that saltwater fly fishermen represent to the fops and mystic brie eaters who dominate the sport's western regions. Or so I believed.

I decided to play along. "You really think I have a shot at winning?" I asked.

"Not a prayer; even if God drops everything else to help," Lokay answered. "The costume competition is your best hope. But remember—this is Vail, and we have standards. Buy underwear."

In terms of status and respectability, undergarments should be last on the list of worries that might plague Colorado's three-point-five million residents, many of whom are immigrant Californians and, therefore, fashion conscious and prone to anxiety. They, and like-minded newcomers, are changing the fabric of

Colorado and the social vestments as well. Driving, for the first time in many years, west from Denver, through the Sawatch snowpeaks, I noticed far fewer pickup trucks racked with Winchesters and Remingtons, but a great increase in the number of Range Rovers, Land Cruisers and Beemers rack-rigged for kayaks, mountain bikes, and fly rods.

I read the clever bumper stickers as they flew past me on I-70, the fast new four lane: "Visualize World Peace"; "Keep Your Fly Dry."

In a state once controlled by stockmen, the Rockies, at least, have become an alternative-lifestyle magnet to telecommuters and modern cowboys; West Coast and East Coast professionals who are stock-smart but have never branded a stray in their lives; men and women who are pioneer minded enough to realize that, as long as they have a fax machine and a cellular phone, they can live next to any national park on Earth and still do business with the wider world. Moreover, direction to their flight has been shepherded by the discovery that a ski pole or fly rod fits as comfortably in their hands as a Frisbee once did.

Not that they, the Radofornians, now dominate the state's spirit—Colorado is too big, too varied for that. Even as I drove toward the Gore Mountain Range, I was confident that, down on the Front Range, Boulder's transcendent were *hara*-deep in aromatherapy, the Denver Think Tank Center was crackling with fresh ways to become the financial titan of the New West, while north, in borderline roustabout towns such as Glennwood Springs and Rangely, certain Old West types were cleaning their varmint rifles, filled with the hope and anticipation that some yupster's poodle would trespass within hollow-point range.

Yes, I was mustering a healthy, competitive cynicism. Still smarting from Lokay's words (". . . if God drops everything else . . ."), I was assembling a kick-butt game face; an angry flat-lander priming himself for the Ironman of Fly Fishing Championship of the World. I carried this foul disposition right into Vail, a Swiss Deco community where the image of jet-set wealth is underscored by local cops who drive Audi patrol cars. Ironically, it was Vail, surprising Vail, that softened my mood. It was October in the Rockies. Geologic cataclysm defined the valley floor: fissures, wood peaks, and sheer rock bluffs—the frozen tumult of a slow, slow topographical clock. There had been snow in the high country. Altitude could be gauged by demarcations of autumn powder that illuminated ski trails among the gray aspens. Winter was working its way down mountains.

But it wasn't just the scenery. I expected the people to be territorial snots. They weren't. They were open and cheerful and full of fun. I took a room at a hotel with the difficult name of Gasthof Gramshammer (after a couple of Coors, it comes out "Gashouse Grandslammer"), then walked along fast-flowing Gore Creek to Glenn Lokay's tackle shop. It was the day before the Ironman, and Lokay, with his Yosemite Sam mustache and malamute eyes, was holding a meeting for contestants. I'd assumed the place would be jammed with A River Runs Through It types (the ten-dollar entry fees were being donated to river conservation). Instead, only about a dozen men and women milled through the shop, mostly Colorado guides. As they listened to Lokay describe the events ("I've only had about a week to plan this thing, so hang loose") they passed a pint of whiskey around, taking time only to spit disgusting Copenhagen loogies out the door.

I thought: *Typical.*

Even so, I had to give the local guides credit—they were as friendly as they were knowledgeable; not a swollen ego among them. Since the actual fishing would be my weakest event, I was touched when several of them went way out of their way to help me choose a fly and leader material for the one-fly fish-off. I also had to give Lokay credit—despite the short notice, he'd wrangled some big-ticket prizes for the winners: gorgeous Sage fly rods and a superb Abel reel, among them. By the end of the meeting, I actually felt penitent for my sweeping and unfair judgments of these amiable and generous people. Maybe I was befuddled by the Jim Beam, maybe it was the damn snuff they fed me, but I really began to wonder if it wasn't I, after all, who was the territorial snot.

The next day, though, the morning of the Ironman, I felt better—steely and full of competitive fire. More like my old self. After all, I hadn't come to this mountain paradise to have fun. It was Lokay who reminded me of the date: Friday the thirteenth. "Good luck," he smiled. "You're going to need it."

Which would have been true . . . if I hadn't already packed my tackle bag with all the luck I needed.

Vail has hosted a garden variety of national and international competitions, not to mention Gerald Ford and the late Princess Di, but never in its short history had the village accommodated an event so outlandish as the Ironman of Fly Fishing Championship of the World—that's what I was thinking as I stood, in my underwear, on the ninth fairway of the Vail Country Club, alternately ducking golf balls and cursing the wing-tipped bastards who whacked them at us.

"Ignore those linksters," Lokay instructed us. "Pretend they're not there. I knew they'd behave like this. Like they *own* the place."

The day was sun bright; the sky a glacial blue. There were eleven of us carrying fly rods, ten men and one woman making practice casts, warming up for the first two events: distance casting and golf. I felt as if my attire was apropos of the occasion. I wore a partisan banner in the form of red Florida State Seminole boxer shorts, plus an old green wrestling singlet beneath. Several of the other contestants wore long johns—a prissy concession to the October chill, I believed, and also a symptom of weak character.

Yes, I was feeling confident. One reason was that I *knew* I was going to win the distance casting. I knew it not because I was the best caster there (frankly, I wasn't) but because a friend of mine, Professor Bruce Richards of Scientific Anglers, had FedExed me a special high-tech fly line, which, the afternoon before, I had consistently thrown 120 feet. (I'd mention the type of line, but some of you are unethical enough to use it against me next year.)

Another reason I felt confident was that I had finagled a buddy of mine, Bobby Cox, into signing up for the competition. A former member of the NHL's Chicago Blackhawks, Cox's journeyman career carried him to every third-rate hockey rink from Stockholm to Kiev, where he slashed capitalist and commie defensemen with equal impunity, and where he earned for himself a dark reputation and a darker nickname: Sideshow Bob. Were the world orderly and rational, scientists would have darted Cox like a bear, then kept him under observation for years before releasing him back into the wild. But the world is neither, and

Cox, now in his mid-forties, has parlayed his contacts and his gift for languages into international holdings and a newer reputation as a financial wizard. (The man lives in Breckenridge, but plays on my Florida men's baseball team, so commutes to games by jet.)

Cox knew nothing about fly fishing, but he was my key to winning the river run. As we stood on the ninth fairway, I told Cox, "I'll win the distance casting, I should place in the golf and the accuracy. The costume competition is anybody's guess . . . say, how do I look?"

"Idiotic. Like a KGB agent who robbed a circus."

"Perfect. Then I've got a chance—as long as you play blocker for me during the river run. No one gets past you, understand? *No one*. Except for me, of course."

Cox wobbled the fly rod he was holding. "How the hell am I supposed to hurt anybody with this? It's not even sharp. You told me fly fishing was *fun*."

I patted him on the shoulder. "Hockey has given you a wonderfully quirky approach to life, Sideshow. But your secret is safe with me. Just get the job done."

Trouble was, I didn't get the job done. Not in the distance casting, anyway. I placed a miserable fourth or fifth, casting only ninety-some feet—but there were legitimate reasons for my sad performance. One was that I expected the Ironman to be a poorly organized debacle, but it wasn't. Lokay brought in popular Littleton guide Bob Jaquess, former mission manager of the Martin Marietta's Titan 4 project, to administer the competition and he ran each event with the precision of a rocket scientist. The shock of that was numbing. Another reason was that some doofus was standing on my line when I made my cast—me, the doofus. However, I rallied during the golf (a hundred-yard par five cast, with a nasty dogleg right) and managed to bogie the hole, as did Gore Creek guides Mike "Poodle Head" Moser and Mike Paderewski. Poodle Head (who cast 106 feet into the wind to win the distance event) and Paderewski (who wore a red union suit with a wooly worm on the fly) would prove to be my strongest competition, although I kicked their respective butts during the eighty-yard, closest-to-the-pin shoot-out to win the golf.

It was at about that point in the competition that Vail guide Jimmy Garrett began to ply the leaders (which didn't include him) with strong drink. For that reason, the next few events are a blur, although I recall that I was accused of cheating during the blindfolded knot tying, and that, as expected, I didn't do too well in the actual one-fly fish-off (I caught two tiny rainbows). Susan Beninati made a strong showing in the accuracy casting (the prettiest event, with casters lined along the river, throwing beautifully tight loops) although it was Poodle Head who won, while I placed second. I also recall that, as we moved from event to event, we began to acquire a crowd of onlookers plus media coverage, which, in Lokay's mind, prophesied well for next year's Ironman and his river conservation charity. This I was glad to see. Lokay had been badly dispirited by my morning successes— "The ironman's reputation will be compromised if a chum-slinger like you places higher than ninth"—but the attention the event was receiving seemed to buoy his mood. "Even your freakish luck can't dent this thing's momentum," he chided just before the final event. "Hundreds will want to sign up next year. We'll have to limit applications."

Undoubtedly. In a social fabric as varied as Colorado's, any colorful, outlandish cross-weave is welcome. I was finally beginning to appreciate that.

What I remember best, though, is the river run (officially, the "Boxer Speed Spawn"). The official overall standings had Poodle Head Moser in first place, me in second (I had added valuable points to my tally by placing third in the costume competition). If I could manage a win, and if Poodle Head did poorly, I would be Ironman of Fly Fishing Champion of the World. The course was intimidating: up the middle of the Eagle River to a sandspit, then across through a chest-deep swale, then back . . . all in near-freezing water, in our underwear.

As we lined the bank, awaiting the start, I nudged Cox, winked at him, and said, "Pretend we're on the blue line, and you've got to stop every Russian in the world from beating you to the goal."

A strange and terrible light came into the man's eyes. "Russians?" he whispered. "You . . . *you* look like a Russian . . ." Which is when the gun sounded . . . and Sideshow Bobby Cox paused only long enough to yank my underwear to my ankles before he splashed off to victory in a rage of elbows and head butts, beating every man and woman there, most of whom were half his age.

Later, when he came to his senses, and while I was inspecting my second-place prize—the Abel reel—Cox would apologize, adding, "You're right. Fly fishing *is* fun."

The Most Dangerous Game

For those of us who exalt in an outdoor challenge, particularly those few of us who, as professionals, not only excel at wilderness skills but are also spiritually in tune ("at one," some say) with nature, it is fated that not only will we one day play paintball, but that we will like it more than we had hoped.

Paintball, you may know, is the sport in which normally peace-loving women, men, and children dress themselves in masks and camo, arm themselves with pneumatic guns, then play nature's oldest game: stalk and conquer. In short, they run around crazily while zapping like-minded hobbyists.

The elements are compelling: fresh air, the camaraderie, the opportunity to be courageous in the face of adversity. Particularly alluring is the atavistic urge to sneak around in the bushes and shoot people.

Who could resist? But that's just what I did. I resisted because of a personal malady and an unfortunate experience in paintball's fledgling days. Years ago, a friend stopped by to demonstrate his new paintball pistol, blasting away at a garbage can. The sound of a paintball gun is distinctive—*whump, whump, whump*—it is similar to the bark of a flatulent pig. But more impressive is the velocity. Paintballs look benign in a bag; little biodegradable spheres filled with water-soluble dye. But when fired, they streak away at a hundred yards per second; pastel tracers that sizzle as they pass one's ear.

"Doesn't that hurt?" I wanted to know.

"Stings a little," my friend said. "Want me to show you?"

"Sure," I said, reaching for his pistol. No telling what I was supposed to learn from such an example, but I was willing to shoot him if he wanted.

"No," he said, "trot down the road and, when you're far enough away, I'll try to hit you in the leg."

"And it'll just sting?"

"Right. Stings just a little."

I trotted. I heard the gun bark. I felt it hit me.

"Ouch! Jesus!"

Which brings us to my personal malady—sympathetic ocular/auditory response, physicians call it. What that means is, if I am slapped or snapped or hit by a paintball, my eyes and nose begin to drip simultaneously so that it appears as if I am weeping.

"My gosh," my fiend said, "it couldn't have hurt that bad."

"You hit me right on the butt!"

"I know, but a grown man—crying."

I wasn't, of course. My pain tolerance is extremely high—toughened by years on the trail spent . . . doing many tough things. Even though the paintball struck me in an extremely sensitive, albeit heavily muscled area, I had barely felt it. But in paintball, as in life, appearance counts for much. Which was why I did not participate as the sport grew around me.

Yet it was inevitable that I would—fated, as I've said. So recently when another friend, a martial arts expert named Bill, explained to me his version of the ultimate game, I listened only out of a sense of responsibility to my own destiny. Then I agreed to play, but for a different reason. Reasons, to be precise; four or five of them, all liquid, all drained from beverage cans—an old martial arts ploy that I will never fall for again.

Bill lives on a heavily wooded island, and he proposed that I come to the island at an agreed upon time, track him, and try to shoot him with a paintball rifle. That sounded like fun. I would be the hunter and he would be the hunted. So far, so good.

But here was the catch—Bill would also have a gun. If he could, he would shoot me first. "Neither of us has played paintball before," he said. "That makes it fair."

Not the way I saw it. The quarry isn't supposed to return fire. Ask any hunter.

But I had agreed, and there was no going back.

Because he knew the island so well, Bill told me that he would drop corn kernels along the way so that I could track him more easily. The game would begin at dusk and go into darkness.

"If you last that long," he added.

Hah! Who did he think he was dealing with? Besides, I had a plan of my own. I wasn't the naive fool he took me for—by the time I got to his island, I'd make sure I had plenty of paintball experience under my belt. If he wanted to believe I was a rank novice, that was his problem.

I'm not going to lie about it. Here's who I expected to find at an organized paintball field: an unattractive cast of frustrated Rambos, some of whom kept pythons as pets, circled their i's, and clipped their horoscopes. They would say things like, "I need the adrenaline head rush," or "That's why I only watch MTV." The type who, if I gave them any guff, would scratch around and piss on my tires.

But it wasn't that way. I went to a field near the town in which I live, and there found about two dozen men and women of various backgrounds but similarly pleasant dispositions. They had all the guns and accompanying gear (paintball has become a multi-million-dollar-a-year business) and I was charmed by the descriptive names: eighty-round E-Z loaders, pro series Zap Balls, Sheridan Piranha, Bloodsucker, Phantom, Bushmaster, Jaguar, Nightmare, Mirage sighting system, direct nipple feeds, ribbed silencer, lighted point sight, Thunderwear gloves, Predator Thermal Goggles. A spritely list that told me these folks were dedicated enthusiasts. They knew their sport. But they weren't too busy to welcome me or my eleven-year-old son, whom I had brought along. They showed us how the guns worked. They demonstrated how to deal with a jammed paintball—not an uncommon occurrence in a hot firefight. They hammered at the safety rules: masks and goggles on at all times, barrel plugs in unless on the field, and, when at close range, the obligation to shout to an opponent "Take a hit?"—a phrase associated only with hipsters two decades ago, but that now has a whole new nineties spin. If the opponent says "Yes!" you are honor bound not to shoot. You can't waste them, wax them, smoke them, or zap them. They have capitulated. They want their nice day to continue.

We played. No single game lasted more than fifteen minutes, so we played all morning. At first it was scary, then it was exhilarating. Because a participant must concentrate so completely upon the task at hand, it will be only another year or two before someone writes about "The Zen of Paintball," and I'm glad we got in under the rope.

I was shot three different times—always by my loving son. Once he asked why my eyes were watering, and I tried to explain that, in a survival situation, it was nature's way of blurring my vision so that I wouldn't have to see what hellish business God had cooked up next.

It was fun. So much fun I wished I had been invited by writers Charles Gaines and Lionel Atwill to play in the world's first paintball match back in the early eighties. Gaines, along with Bob Gurnsey and Hayes Noel, founded an industry when, on a lark, they armed a bunch of their buddies with stock-marking guns (normally used by veterinarians) and took their survival game to the woods.

"I didn't invite you because I didn't know you," Gaines would tell me later. "And now that I do know you, I'm pretty sure we wouldn't have invited you, anyway."

Masters of the friendly barb, those founding fathers of paintball.

But I had my own personal survival game going now. Just me and the martial arts expert, Bill. I had already assured myself of one advantage—a whole morning under fire. Good solid paint-ball experience. But I wasn't going to stop there. Preparation was the key. So I bought my own gun, a P68 Piranha long barrel; a sinister-looking top-of-the-line pump gun that would blast paint just as fast as I could shuck the slide. And a neat-looking face mask, too. My son said I looked like Arnold Schwarzenegger when I modeled it around the house.

"Around the eyes," he said. "Just a little bit."

Perfect. The match was only a day away. And I was ready to kung-fu kick a little keister.

Bill didn't study kung fu. I remembered that as I pulled up to his boat dock the evening of our shoot-out. It was something else; one of those esoteric branches of discipline—kendo, that was it. Japanese sword fighting. Or saber fighting. I wasn't sure. But it was something that required him to wear a suit of black armor. A Japanese Darth Vader, that's what the armor resembled. It had startled me, the first time I saw it stacked in his study. An evil-looking black helmet with segmented body shields: a cyborg crus-tacean with rows of fighting swords mounted on the wall above it. Exactly the kind of thing he would wear in this contest with the hopes of frightening me—an absurd gambit that made me smile.

I decided to try to lure him out: "Hello? Anybody home? Want to have a beer first?"

No answer.

It's eerie landing on an island at dusk. Bill's house was empty—no lights, no movement. He was already back in the jungle someplace, just as he said he would be at this hour. Waiting for me to stalk him. I checked my watch. Seven-fifteen, so he already had a fifteen-minute head start. He was probably already dug in, up in one of those coconut palm or gumbo limbo thickets waiting to ambush me.

Fine. That's what it was all about. Man against man. A war of nerves and steel—well, nerves and water-soluble dye, anyway. Precisely the kind of challenge I live for.

But I decided to let him stew for a while. I checked the lines of my boat, I checked my gear. My Piranha pump gun was ready to rock and roll. Plenty of gas in the seven-ounce constant-feed cylinder, fifty fresh .68-caliber paintballs in the magazine. For the first time, I wished I had invested in some camouflage clothing. Still, my red baseball jersey didn't seem a bad choice. If, for only an instant, he confused me with a lost and drunken church league softball player, he was as good as dead.

I called toward the woods: "The mosquitoes seem unusually bad, don't they? Maybe we should postpone, play in the afternoon so we can see what the hell we're doing?"

A final attempt to lure him into the open so that I could zap him at my leisure. But my firm invitation was absorbed by the foliage and vanished into the creaking, chirping silence.

It was dark now. I moved past Bill's house into the thicket beyond. Paths sprayed away in several directions. I chose the widest of them, reasoning that, if I had to make a forced retreat, there was less chance of stumbling over a log. With me I carried a little magnum penlight and, every so often, I checked the trail.

It didn't take me long to find Bill's spore: *Corn.* A handful of kernels dropped in a pile, translucent yellow in the light. Quickly, I moved several paces ahead and found more—I was definitely on his trail.

I switched off the flashlight and dropped down into the tall grass to think. Bill could be a quarter mile ahead . . . or a hundred yards . . . or ten yards. No way of knowing, and it would be stupid to follow his trail into a trap. Idiotic. Even painful.

Right.

Without hesitating, I backtracked, then headed off in the opposite direction. Once safely away, I began to walk more quickly. I thought I would intersect with the trail that I had followed originally, but I didn't. I shined the light around. No house. No boat dock. But I couldn't be lost. Impossible. It was just so darn dark.

I stopped and knelt to check my compass. Only I couldn't find my compass. Well, maybe I had dropped it. I used the flashlight to look . . . and saw another pile of corn at my feet.

Hmmm . . .

I switched out the light and dropped to my belly, gun ready. I lay and waited, all my senses straining to find some sign of Bill . . . or, better yet, the boat dock. One of them had to be close, and I was hoping it was the boat dock. But I wasn't going to move. Not again. No, that would be playing right into his hands. Let him come looking for me.

Nothing. I couldn't see anything, and I couldn't hear anything but crickets and cicadas and the distant churring of an owl. It was quiet. Just like in the cowboy movies: too quiet. As I lay there, I began a methodical review of the situation. It was true I wasn't lost, but it was also true that I had no idea where I was. Okay, I could deal with that because I had been in similar spots many times before. But what about Bill? Sure, we had fished together a few times, but just how well did I really know the guy?

Not well, that's what I decided.

I knew he spent a lot of time lifting weights, I knew he studied kung fu . . . well, kendo. One of those Oriental blood sports where students pretend they don't really want to kill anyone, but spend years learning exactly how to do it just in case. Some hobby! And what kind of person would live alone on an island? True, the island was connected to the mainland by a bridge, and there were a few others who chose to live on the island—but not more than six or seven thousand people. The nearest 7-Eleven was fifteen miles away, for God's sake. Clearly, there was something antisocial in such behavior, for there was nothing to do out here but watch movies and practice sword fighting—if one happened to be twisted enough to own swords.

For me, lying there alone in the darkness, that's when the whole situation came into focus. *Movies.* Bill loved movies. He watched them all the time. Then I remembered a movie I had seen once, *The Most Dangerous Game*, starring Joel McCrae. In that film, McCrae, who lived on an island, invited people out so that he could hunt and kill them. Had he used a sword? I couldn't remember. But shave McCrae's head and give him big muscles, and he and Bill could have been twins.

Paintball, indeed! Finally, I understood just what I had gotten myself into. I was alone, on an island, with a Joel McCrae freak who, at this very moment, was probably stalking around in a Darth Vader suit, carrying a bag of corn in one hand and probably a sword in the other. No doubt chanting some evil Oriental mantra, too, whipping his karma into a murderous frenzy.

Well, he'd have to catch me first!

I jumped to my feet and took off jogging. There was nothing panicky in my movements. I knew precisely what I had to do. Coolly, calmly, I had to run and run and run until I found my boat, or drop from exhaustion trying. Escape was the only rational option and, if nothing else, I am a rational man.

I ran for a long way. Many minutes. I stopped once to listen, shining the light. That's when I saw it . . . more corn.

Mother of God, had Amish invaded the island?

I began to move slowly backward, watching, listening. That's when I heard a soft, homicidal whisper: *"Take a hit?"*

I was so startled that I swung around instinctively while my Piranha pump gun belched paint.

Then I heard: "Ouch! Jesus! I'm hit!"

It was Bill. He came stumbling out of the bushes, shining his own flashlight at his chest, his arms. He wasn't wearing his kendo armor—maybe he'd ditched it somewhere, along with his sword. For now he wore a gray T-shirt and bandana, and carried a PGP paint pistol—a nice weapon, but no match for my long-barreled repeater. "Hey," he said, "your paintball didn't break. I'm not really hit."

Too late. I knew the rules. He had called a hit, and that was the game. I won.

On the path back to the house, he told me, "I have to give you credit. You didn't follow a single false trail. Everywhere I went, you were right with me, man. How'd you do that?"

I remember saying something modest. Something about, if I told him all my bushwhacking secrets, the entire Japanese Empire would know within days.

He said, "What? Oh yeah—ha-ha."

Let him laugh. Who did he think he was dealing with?

I am, after all, an outdoors professional.

Surfer's Rule

O f late, my ears have been reconfiguring the familiar: The bell notes of blue jays sound like sea buoys; passing cars assume the cadence of distant surf. Over on the East Coast, in Melbourne, Florida,—one hundred forty miles from my home—David Hamilton is shaping one of his Vector boards for me. Through my office window, I can hear his brush strokes in the oaks.

On the phone, Dave tells me that a guy my age, my size, definitely needs a long board. He says, "A long board, that's the way to go." I tell Dave, yeah, a long board—precisely what I want. As I speak, I picture the board: Corvette-bright with pinstripes; a biconic shape that would not seem out of place if spiked into a bluff on Easter Island.

Dave tells me that he's going to build the board with an extra tail rocker, three stringers, and a long panel V to facilitate rail-to-rail turns—plus, the thinner rails will make it easier to keep an edge in the face of a wave.

I don't know a rocker from a rail, but I answer, "Absolutely. The thinner the rails, the better."

"And you want it glossed and polished, right?" Before I can answer, he's describing the process: careful sanding; all pores sealed with rubbing compound and ebony wax; then hand buffed.

I picture Dave laboring over the board—he's 6'6", salt-bleached hair hangs to the middle of his back—and I see the material come to life beneath his hands. The skin of the board throbs, flickers. The man has been shaping since the sixties; started in his Miami backyard, moved to California and opened a shop near Encinitas; ended up in Melbourne, now forty-four, still wearing flip-flops and Hawaiian shirts; still closing shop when surf is pumping. Who am I to question a veteran?

"Of course," I tell Dave, "glossed and polished."

He says, "Oh yeah—and I'll create a mild nose concave to facilitate nose riding."

I picture myself crouched on the board, pursued by a wall of water, hair streaming as I tightrope toward the nose: an illustration of control on a wave that communicates random momentum.

". . . which is why," Dave explains, "I'm recommending a nine-six. 'Cause of the extra flotation? A guy your size and age, you're really going to need it."

Why does he have to keep saying that?

The imagination blurs; the wave collapses—I no longer tightrope, my hair no longer streams. These days, I am reminded, I don't have enough hair to sop water.

Surfer's Rule

Dave says, "If that's the board you want, I can build it. But it'll cost some money."

I tell Dave, "Do it."

I am forty-five years old and weigh 220 pounds. Friends and family have been selecting delicate, convoluted routes to tell me that I am too old, too bearish to learn to surf. I accept the finesse as a measure of their affection. They refer to my knees—haven't thirty-some years of baseball, squatting behind the plate, atrophied necessary quickness? They mention my back—a biking accident in the Bahamas resulted in a fourth lumbar that is as treacherous as a chained dog. What if I suffer a seizure while in the surf?

"All it *takes* is one wave," a doctor friend warns me.

I prefer to alter the inflection, so that his warning becomes a dictum: All it takes is *one* wave.

I've been anticipating that wave for longer than he knows; for longer than I should have allowed myself to wait.

Here's a flash: Years roll by.

For more than thirty-two years, I have been catching surrogate waves, and enough's enough. I'm thinking of a farm house, seven miles from a microscopic grange town that you won't find on any atlas. My room was upstairs with a window that faced west. I spent a lot of years viewing the world from altitude: pear tree, garden, windscapes of corn; sunsets and new moons. At night, my radio picked up WLS Chicago, and sometimes WBZ Boston—the outer perimeters of human contact. I heard a song: "Surfin' USA." With haying money, I bought the album and a record player. I heard another song: "In My Room." I'd leave the window open and listen to the music, feeling the sanctuary, absorbing a westwarding wind.

Another covert surfer was talking to me, telling me something. One night—it was late—my buddy Alan Ring called with an outrageous story: Parked outside Becker's Restaurant, downtown, was a car, he said, with *California license plates*.

"You're lying," I said.

"I'm not. Trust me!"

The last time Alan had urged me to trust him was when he tried to convince me to stick my tallywhacker into the tubes of a milking machine. He claimed to have been doing it for months with startling results.

I got my bike from the barn and flew back roads into town. No lights, no traffic; nothing but corn stubble and isolated house lights set way back in. It was cold, and I wondered: Why would anyone from California come to northwestern Ohio?

I never found out. But the car was there, a red Corvette, gold-on-blue license plates, and some kind of strange rack on the back. Two guys, early twenties, sat inside Becker's, reading menus while, outside, locals demonstrated their fascination by affecting a rural indifference.

I remember a portion of conversation:

"What's that rack for?"

"Their *boards*, you dope."

"Boards? Jesus Christ, why would anybody carry lumber on a car like that?"

I sat on my bike listening, watching the Californians through the illuminated frame of window, hoping to God they didn't order the local milk.

They drank Cokes with their hamburgers. They were lean and blond—a genetic anomaly, in my experience—and wore chambray shirts and jeans. They appeared tired. They ignored us. One of the local girls strolled by their booth, hoping to goad an introduction. They ignored her, too. My confidence drained—there were things I wanted to ask. Were they from Hawthorn, California? Did they know Brian Wilson?

I'd positioned my bike so that they had to walk past me to get to their car. This shyness of ours was chafing, all the more so because it seemed to bloom from the marrow—yet our credentials were a matter of public record. The previous season, hadn't our high school baseball team placed second in the state? Lost 1–0, down there in Columbus, taking the big schools right to the wall. Could hicks do that?

As they exited the restaurant, I waited. They brushed past us, insulating themselves from our stares with conversation. I tried to make eye contact; didn't. Tried to say hello; couldn't. But as they were getting into their car, I finally found voice, asking the only question that I could think to ask: "Do you guys surf?"

The Californian on the passenger side peered up from the bucket seat and allowed a patient smile. It was as if I had asked if the world were round, and yet, I believed, there was also something fraternal in his expression; an acknowledgment of acceptance for no other reason than I knew the word. As he closed the door, he answered me—"Fuckennay, man"—and then they drove off, popping through the gears, laying a yelp of rubber in third just to show us, and I watched the Corvette with the California plates meld with the highway, and then distance, mesmerized by the potential of a road that really could be ridden from there to anywhere.

This was in 1963, when I was thirteen. It was November, a month easy to recall.

There are things that can be owned which, through design or association, also represent aspirations that cannot be purchased. I have a friend whose garage is a trophy room of climbing gear. My wife puts her running medals in a drawer, but arranges her Nikes as carefully as a row of candles. Personally, things that come to mind are a Sea Master fly reel, a Wilson Pro-Toe catcher's glove, a Hewes flats skiff, and a custom surfboard. Concerning the latter: I have yet to take delivery.

David Hamilton says it'll take three weeks, maybe more. Something about getting just the right blank. I tell him, "No rush." After postponing the acquisition for more than two decades, what's a month? To me, this slow approach to a thing I've always wanted to do is not puzzling, yet I can offer no simple explanation. Surfing, as I perceived it, was not among those sports that could be bagged like game. It accommodated too many dynamics to be attacked. Surfing had to be encountered, waited upon until the time was right. There was pleasure in believing that the moment would come.

Here are things I never expected, anticipated, or associated with surfing: Oneness with All Things, Mother Ocean, Mother Nature, Mother Earth, Flipper, mood rings, perfect waves.

Here are a few things that I do associate with surfing and find attractive because of overtones and depth of inference: highways, seascapes, California in the seventies, Sex Wax, "Pet Sounds," the potential of undiscovered places, and the precise wave seismology of distant winds; summer nights, small American towns, small wars in which Charlie didn't surf.

I read surf magazines, kept up on the controversies. Would long boards be eclipsed by super-short, tube-ripping plastic machines? Would grommets and ho-daddies and surf Nazis ruin it all for the few True Surfers? And what about those new goon cords, or ankle leashes? Was the purity of the sport being compromised?

A year didn't pass that I was not waiting.

The question is: Have I waited too long?

The first time I paddled out into big surf, a board beneath me, I was certain that I had. There are ambient factors that those of us who have ridden only surrogate waves choose to ignore: Surfing is among the most physically demanding sports; surfers may be the most underrated athletes in the world; paddling alone through a screaming tide rip and breaking surf is scary as hell— an existential prologue that scatters romance like so much chafe and leaves the pretender quaking like an aspen leaf.

Me, the pretender.

I got hammered; I got dumped and spun until I didn't know which way was up—unpleasant when one is underwater. Once, I lost purchase in the belly of a wave, and the board whacked me so hard in the face that I saw cartoon starbursts. I not only couldn't catch a wave, I apparently couldn't even make it out beyond the reef break. Later, when a friend told me that I had resembled a gorilla trying to drown a Popsicle stick, I thought: How can she be so flippant? Doesn't she know that this is important?

This was several months ago at a surf spot called Beacon's, thirty miles north of San Diego, when the weather was right, the mood was right, and, it seemed to me, the handwriting was on the wall. I had come to San Diego for other reasons, so an oblique encounter with surfing was ideally fitted to my perceptions. More to the point, I genuinely believed that it was now or never.

I had read that surfing was one of the few sports that could not be taught. I found that attractive. The timing, the balance, the ability to read waves were not linear components like a golf swing. They couldn't be related; they could only be absorbed. Even so, someone in San Diego told me about a man who taught surfing; that I could find him under "K" in the phone book— Kahuna Bob Edwards. Kahuna (it's impossible to call him anything else) told me that, in the last nine years, he had taught more than three thousand people to surf, including men who were older and larger than I. We met the next morning at La Jolla Shores where, on a soft foam board, he demonstrated the basics. This was in waist-deep water with a gentle beach break. Kahuna, middle aged and athletic, made it look easy. Surfers always make surfing look easy. I floundered around for an hour, but couldn't manage to stand. It was maddening. My first attempt at snow skiing, I went down the mountain; my first time in a kayak, I made it down the river. Surfing required more. Toward the end of the lesson, I got briefly to my feet, then crashed off the board into the sand.

I'd done it; I'd surfed—or so I told myself. But it was a lie, and the lie grated on me over the next few days, which is why I called Kahuna Bob again, and how I ended up at Beacon's fighting for my life in a screaming riptide that cleaved eight-foot faces off ocean rollers before toppling them onto rocks. I wanted to try the real thing. Beacon's was the real thing.

Kahuna put me on an old tandem board that he called The Beast, selected a board for himself, and I tried to follow him out through the surf. I kept dumping the board. When I was engorged with salt water, exhausted, Kahuna paddled back and yelled, "We're almost outside the break. It's *nice* out there!"

It *was* nice out there. When I'd finally made it, I sat and looked shoreward. It was like floating on the liquid membrane of some great respiratory system. The beach would rise out of the sea, dilate into a golden border, then vanish as I watched the back side of breakers sail past. It was so nice, so peaceful, that I was reluctant to return to the rim of the break, yet, that is the essence of surfing: to goad oneself into a position to be swept away. I did—and got thrashed. Tried it a second time and felt my right groin muscle tear. Had I not been so frightened of paddling back through the breakers, I wouldn't have tried a third time, but I did. I felt a wave inflate beneath me . . . felt the sudden transfer of velocity as the board gathered buoyancy . . . almost tumbled as I got to my feet—but caught myself . . . and then I was standing . . . *standing* . . . gaining speed as the cliffs of Encinitas rushed toward me, viewing the world from altitude . . . and I rode the wave a hundred yards or more, all the way to the beach where a woman with salt-bleached hair, wearing a black wet suit, stood watching. She may have thought me mad the way I, a stranger, hobbled toward her, calling, "Did you see that? *Did* you? That was my first wave!"

She had a wonderful face; her expression was amused, fraternal, and distantly familiar. She grinned and said, "Yeah, I saw! Man, you're really *stoked.*"

The next week, I called David Hamilton.

My surfboard now leans against an office bookcase. It is candy-gloss white with Corvette pinstriping. Near the nose, the "VEC-TOR" logo is backdropped by a line drawing of the world. I like that. I am also pleased by the board's shape. It would not be out of place if spiked into any ancient hillside anywhere on that map.

I am less heartened, however, by my recent attempts to catch a wave. I took delivery of the board two weeks ago and spent the next few days on Florida's east cost, morning until night, being humiliated by Atlantic winter surf. Not once did I get to my feet for more than a millisecond.

Late yesterday afternoon, I drove to Captiva, a Florida west coast island, in hopes of taking advantage of surf created by forty-knot winds. In a parking lot, the wind ripped my board off the roof and it hit a rental car in which were two big German women—a circumstance never anticipated by Brian Wilson, so never idealized by The Beach Boys. The police were called; it was getting late. I used sign language to tell the women I was going into the water. They demanded to keep my driver's license until I returned. It seemed petty. Actually it was smart. Once outside the breakers, the wind blew me like a leaf into a tidal rip that carried me out to sea. Tourists lined the bridge to watch this Real-Life Drama. It was after sunset before I finally battled my way to the next island, happy to be alive, but absurdly distressed that I had not gotten a shot at a single wave. The Germans were unsympathetic. The sheriff's deputy (an occasional surfer) couldn't have been kinder. "Maybe your board blew off for a reason," he suggested.

Well, maybe . . .

Fight it as I might, it is impossible to approach even the periphery of the sport without being swept into venues that take karmas seriously. It may be because surfing is the hardest thing in the world. At Beacon's, after riding The Beast clear to shore, I walked to the top of the bluff and met Rod Aries, a big guy in his forties who is a former ballplayer turned surfer. Aries, a financial consultant, owned the house across the street; checking the break was a morning ceremony. When I told him about my first wave, he shook his head with mock sadness and said, "It's all downhill from here, buddy." Even so, he continues to prod me along via e-mail. He once wrote: ". . . in baseball you follow the flight of the ball and you experience it from afar. In surfing you are the flight of the ball and experience it firsthand."

Surfers say things like that. It can't hurt just to listen.

TWO

AN AMERICAN TRAVELER

A Train, America, and a Frog

1

Item in Amtrak's Express Magazine: *Nearly every 48 hours, motorist impatience or inattention causes a vehicle collision with an Amtrak train. On board, Amtrak passengers seldom feel more than a bump. But it can be far more serious for the motorist.*

I find the above interesting because after a day aboard Amtrak's new transcontinental passenger train, the *Sunset Limited*, I have noticed more than a few bumps. Nothing uncomfortable. Just the occasional *ka-THUMP* inserted into the lulling and steady *humpity-humpity-humpity-humpity* of the diesel engine spiriting us across the nation. Sealed within my deluxe sleeper, even the riverboat wail of the train's whistle is hushed, so the unexpected ka-THUMPS are felt more than heard; staccato jolts that interrupt the metronomic swaying of the train.

After reading *Express* magazine, I begin to wonder what kind of automotive debris we might be dragging beneath us. After all, it has been nearly ten hours since I boarded in Winter Haven, Florida, bound for Los Angeles. Statistically, we've had a fair shot at intersecting with a Toyota or two, or perhaps a souped-up Chevy run amok at some country crossing. As I consider the possibilities, Mr. Graham, the attendant, taps at my cabin door. After he takes my dinner reservation, I ask him if, in his thirteen years on the job, he has ever been aboard a train that hit a car. Mr. Graham does not hesitate. "Oh, yes sir, many times, sir. But it's nothing you need to worry about. We don't feel much of anything up here." Up here meaning the upper deck of a superliner car where everything—observation car, dining car, my sleeper— is elevated fifteen feet above the Earth.

So it was possible that we had already hit a car?

"Not this trip. You'll know if we hit a car because we got to sit around while the wrecker hauls the thing off the track. Then we got to call the attorneys. Just getting the coroner out takes two, three hours sometimes." Mr. Graham's expression shares with me the frustrations of trying to maintain a railroad schedule in an unappreciative, unpredictable jet-age America.

Because I enjoy riding trains, I am empathetic. "Yeah, those coroners. It all pays the same to them."

When I am not chatting with Mr. Graham, and when I am not in the dining car joking with the waiters, or when I am not in the observation car meeting fellow passengers, I join my traveling companion in our cabin where I watch the American South roll by. Thus far, the American South has consisted of whistle-stops at Kissimmee, Orlando, Palatka, Tallahassee, and a dozen other Florida towns, most of it Magic Kingdom tourist sprawl and orange grove country. The stops inspire little comment from me, and none from my companion. I have seen it before, for I am a Floridian, and my companion is indifferent, because he is a frog—a Southern bullfrog, to be precise; a fully grown saddle back, as the old-time giggers in the Everglades call large frogs, and I am taking him to California to compete in the Calaveras County Jumping Frog Contest.

But that is another story.

For now we are riding the westbound *Sunset Limited*, routed through Alabama, Mississippi, Louisiana, Texas, then along the Mexican border into New Mexico, Arizona, and California. We are on the port side of Car 130, Room E, a cabin as practical and efficient as the cabin of a good boat. There is a sink, a hose shower in the head, a bunk above, and settee that pulls out into a bed. The outboard wall is nearly six feet of double-thick Margard glass, so I spend most of my time in the chair by the window, reading and watching the countryside roll by. The frog, along with a dozen live crickets, stays in a Tupperware box, where I hope all of them will remain for the duration of this three-day trip. The Amtrak literature does not mince words when it comes to pets. They are "expressly prohibited," and, while it could be argued that a bullfrog is not a pet, it has always been my philosophy that it is easier to apologize than it is to ask permission.

So we sit in our cabin, a quiet cell in a honeycomb of sleepers. Our car is the last of ten cars, all linked to a pair of robotic-looking locomotives—the overall effect of which is to feel a part of some elemental force that displaces great volumes of air as the landscape slides past.

From this elevated vantage point, the mundane, the less mobile, the clotted car traffic, and the stranded townspeople, all seem as temporal, or as trivial, as just another bump on the tracks.

Not counting the frog, there are more than three hundred passengers aboard this train; seats are booked months in advance, so we were very lucky to get a Deluxe Sleeper, though I would have settled for a Family Sleeper, or even an Economy Sleeper. What I didn't want was to spend three nights in a reclining coach seat, shoulder to elbow with a bunch of strangers who, I feared, would demonstrate as little sympathy for my lifelong insomnolence as my choice of traveling companions. I know from experience that, by day, the cost of a sleeper seems extravagant but, come three in the morning, it is the last nickel bargain in town. In the dining car last night, I was seated with Mark and Anne of Clearwater, Florida, an attractive, athletic couple who have taken a break in their routine of jogging, cycling, and all-around healthy living to travel by coach car to New Orleans. This morning when I saw them at breakfast, though, they hardly seemed to be the same people. They appeared gaunt, unsteady, and bleary eyed, as if haunted by the coronas of lights.

"It was hellish," Mark said, describing the night he and his wife had spent. "We were right by the door. It kept opening and closing, opening and closing. I hate that door! I tried to drink myself to sleep, but even that didn't work."

Anne told me, "When we get to our hotel in New Orleans, it's straight to bed."

I said very little. They seemed too frail to endure gloating, and I had had a great night. After a steak dinner, I decided to forego the movie in the observation coach (a car walled and roofed

with windows) as well as bingo in the club car. Instead, I
returned to my sleeper, fed the frog, then showered. There was a
bucket of ice thoughtfully stocked by Mr. Graham, so I dug out a
can of beer and sat with lights off, by the window. The observation car is fine by day; a fun place to eavesdrop and meet fellow
travelers, but nightfall is a more intimate time, particularly on a
train, and I wanted to enjoy it alone. There was no moon, so the
few vignettes of landscape visible were isolated and set apart by
the darkness: the arc of a basketball on a deserted playground; a
woman framed by a lighted window, stretching to brush her hair;
the truckstop haze of the cities and small towns, Pensacola and
Myrtle Grove; the deep South gloom of pine forest that, by dark-
ening my window, allowed previous images to linger for a time,
flickering and fading like dying fires. Traveling at night by train,
the sense of motion and the sense of time are transposed, so
there is a growing illusion that you are a stationary observer of
those who exist beyond the window—and their lives are speed-
ing past at a terrible velocity.

I slept well. A train may be the best place in the world to
sleep, because movement is the lone antidote for a restless spirit.
The only interruption I had was after I switched on a light to
read, and Mr. Graham tapped at the door and poked his head in.
"You need an extra blanket? More ice?"

I told him I was fine.

The attendant paused for a moment, his expression slowly
describing puzzlement. "Say," he said finally, "do you hear that?
Sounds like . . . crickets."

In the frog's box, the crickets were singing their death song—
but I couldn't tell Mr. Graham about that.

I nodded toward the window. "I think we must be passing a swamp."

Mr. Graham considered that for a moment, unconvinced. Then he said, "That's right; that's right, we are. Be due to cross the river into Mobile pretty soon. The crickets are out tonight!"

People who are devoted to physical integrity and personal fitness may find the sedentary life aboard a train irksome—even I was beginning to feel a little stodgy. So when it was announced that we would have a two-hour layover in New Orleans, I put on shorts and running shoes and jogged out of Union Terminal, past the Superdome, toward the French Quarter. But running at midday in New Orleans is not easy. The air is as heavy as hot silk, and every block is spiced with the odor of a different restaurant, each a temptation. After about ten minutes of intensive exercise, I decided I had earned a light meal so, on St. Charles Street, I stepped into the Pearl Restaurant, a working-class bistro with linoleum floors, high ceiling fans, and a lunch counter. Chuck was working behind the bar, and he recommended oysters. I had a dozen, raw. Chuck observed that it was a shame I didn't have time to try the fried oysters, because they were very good, too. I did have time, so I had a dozen of those, plus a bottle of local beer, Dixie Amber Light. I sat there eating and talking with Chuck (people at the Pearl were wonderfully chatty—uncommon in busy, big-city restaurants) so I chose to prolong my stay by ordering a plate of red beans. Chuck served the beans smoking hot, with cornbread and a thick cut of sausage, and he placed another iced bottle of beer on the counter. After the beans, I was trying to choose between an order of seafood gumbo or Miss

A Train, America, and a Frog

Leola's jambalaya when Chuck mentioned that they had just taken a bucket of Cajun boiled potatoes from the cooler, and would I like to try a couple on the house?

I was midway through my second potato, still conversing with Chuck, when I happened to notice that the clock on the wall didn't match the watch on my wrist. To my horror, I realized that last night I had mistakenly backed my watch two hours, not one, when adjusting for the time zone change—instead of having more than an hour to get back to the train, I had less than ten minutes. With the barest of explanations, I threw a wad of money on the counter and bolted out into the heat. To make the train, I would have to sprint the whole way, but I couldn't sprint for long, not after the lunch I had just eaten. Indeed, just *breathing* was uncomfortable. Even so, I struggled along, probably looking like some godforsaken refugee with my distended belly and Quasimodo gait. At the Superdome, I steeled myself and ran the rest of the way to Union Terminal and arrived just in time to hear, "Last call for the *Sunset Limited!*" There were two long lines of people, tickets in hand, waiting to be checked into the boarding area, but I ran seemingly unnoticed right past them and the ticket punchers, proving, perhaps, that joggers have finally joined the ranks of winos and stray dogs as invisible creatures of the street.

As I closed my cabin door, the train began to jolt, then gather speed, and, moments later, Mr. Graham knocked, then asked, "You want me to bring lunch to your cabin?"

I said, "Dear God, no." Even the slightest movement on my part, I feared, would introduce Mr. Graham to the lunch I had just eaten.

"You been out running, that's good. Skip a meal and exercise. Being healthy, that's my man!"

Later, when I could move, I told Mr. Graham about almost being late for the train. He was not surprised. "New Orleans, that's a train-missing town. Happens most every trip."

This trip, too, I learned. Three people missed the train, and they will have to fly to San Antonio to reboard.

The Mississippi River Delta expands with the progress of the *Sunset Limited,* disappearing then seeping to view again in the rum-dark swamps of Bayou LaFourche, New Iberia, and Lafayette. There is a heaviness about the landscape implied by the heat and a mire of silence so tangible that it seems to slow the train. Only the cemeteries radiate sunlight—the white-washed crypts are dazzling in their domino rows—and they pass rhythmically, plastic flowers growing pink and blue from the water-saturated earth. But the cemeteries, like the towns, are outposts. Swamps dominate. Their caverns of cypress and moss are moody, inexorable. Western Louisiana still reflects the character of its own geography—a rarity in Interstate America—and each time we pass an isolated stilt shack or a boat dock of hewn limbs, I wish that I could hop off and get to know the crayfisher-men and crabbers who still make their living from the bayous; share a few meals or a Saturday night beer stop before they, too, are assimilated and finally eliminated by the pasteurization of a nervous America. They are different. They can't last. They will be absorbed as surely as this train absorbs time and distance.

Sunset is delayed by our westward progress but, finally, dusk catches us and soon we are again tunneling through darkness.

A Train, America, and a Frog

We make a whistle-stop in Houston but, even though I know we are now in Texas, the weight and stillness of Louisiana lingers. It seems we have passed through a half dozen decades instead of covering only a few hundred miles. The intensity of the impression is puzzling . . . until I realize that I have, perhaps, confused the effects of the bayous with the nature of train travel itself. Not since plane commerce became commonplace has any city willingly grown up alongside a railroad track. No developer in his right mind would situate a planned community within earshot of diesel horn because no monied buyer in his right mind would live there. Trains have become repellent, yet the very track upon which I travel was once the conduit of modern times. This was the route of choice for high-finance tycoons, movie stars, presidents, big-band musicians, major league baseball teams, and soldiers mustering for war. But the track is a museum piece now; a cross-country corridor frozen in the 1940s, at the peak of its ascendancy. Time can be gauged only by the decline of the derelict towns and factory housing through which we pass. This train has created its own bayous and backwaters. The stillness does not linger. The stillness is decades old, and it echoes.

The dining car seats seventy-two at a serving, four to a table, so each meal I eat with three new people—which means that I am already on a friendly, first-name basis with nearly two dozen fellow passengers. Now, when I pass one of them in the observation car, or meet one downstairs at the snack bar, they unfailingly ask one of two questions. The most common question is, "You think we'll ever get out of Texas?" which is their way of joking about the monotony of the landscape.

For myself, I like Texas. I like the space and the light, and the way cloud shadows gather speed, sailing across the yellow plains. I like the look of the one-windmill ranch houses and the way, in this dry country, the passage of a pickup truck can be marked by its trail of dust. It is a land so desolate that the isolated strongholds of human existence assume worth and a heightened interest. From each infrequent house, children come running out to wave at our train and, an hour ago, in the middle of nowhere, a woman paused beneath a clothesline to catch my eye and smile—or so I choose to believe, for she was very pretty in her flowered dress. Her face was lean and wind blushed, and the unaffected way she tossed her straw hair back communicated an attitude of weathered acceptance. She lived in a mobile home with a fence and a clothesline, and she could still smile at a train. To me, she is one of the many things attractive about Texas, and a reason that I do not answer the question, "You think we'll ever get out of Texas?"

A question I do answer (though I'm always taken aback when it is asked) is, "How's your frog doing?" I have been asked that nine or ten times in the course of the day; clearly, word has gotten out, and I have only myself to blame. When I started the trip, I thought it would be fun to ask people I met along the way to help me name the frog—not that I believe amphibians should be named, I don't. It has been my experience that frogs revel in anonymity, and I had no desire to degrade my jumping frog or his species. Still, asking new friends to suggest a name seemed a way to allow them to share my journey, so that's what I did. Anne and Mark thought Chief Osceola was a good name. "After the famous Florida Indian chief," Anne explained. William, an

A Train, America, and a Frog

Australian I met in the dining car, thought I should call the frog
Roo. "Roo as in kangaroo," he said. "You ever seen those bastards
jump?" A woman who boarded in New Orleans said I should
name the frog Huey P. Long. "Long jump—get it?" I complimented
each suggestion warmly, for the names said more about the
namer than the frog, which is what I had hoped in the first
place. Still, I have yet to use a name when addressing the frog for
the simple reason that I have had no cause, or desire, to speak
with it.

Tonight I did have cause to speak with the frog.

Twice a day, I open the Tupperware box to change the frog's
towel, soaking it first with spring water so that the frog will stay
cool and damp. Then I toss in a few crickets—always wordlessly,
for the frog's stoicism does not inspire conversation. He sits
motionless, his throat pouch pulsing steady as a heartbeat, and
he still does not move when I reseal the lid. Which is why,
tonight, I decided to see if I could make him jump. I was taking
him to a famous jumping frog contest, after all, but since acquir-
ing him from a Florida swamp, I had yet to see the damn thing
move. So I placed the towel on the floor, placed the frog on the
towel, then sat back to gauge his athletic ability.

Nothing. The frog sat there, yellow-eyed and indifferent.

I touched his back legs, and still he did not move.

For the first time, I spoke to the frog: "Three thousand miles
on a train just so you can embarrass me and the whole state of
Florida! Come on, jump!"

I turned to get the bottle of water—maybe he needed dampen-
ing—but when I turned back, the frog was gone. That quick, he

had disappeared. I looked under the bed, under the chair, looked in the shower, even looked in the Tupperware box. No frog. When I saw that I had left my cabin door open, I got down on my hands and knees and crawled out into the hall, which is when I realized with a dawning sense of dread that there was a two-inch crack beneath the door of every sleeper—my frog could easily slip into any room on the train.

I didn't panic. After another careful search of my own quarters, I went to get help. Within minutes, William from Australia was crawling around the west end of the coach and Celeste, of Louisiana, was duck walking the east end, shining a little flashlight. The situation was compromising enough, but then I heard William call, "Roo? Where are ya Roo?!" and, from the other end, I hear Celeste urging, "Oh, Huey-y-y. Come here, Huey-y-y."

I got their attention and held my finger to my lips. William nodded as if he understood, but he didn't understand because, in a softer voice, he began to call, "Roo-o-o? Show yerself, ya bloody little reptile!"

Terrible. I pictured Mr. Graham arriving unexpectedly and demanding an explanation. I pictured us being put off the train—and New Mexico is no place for a frog. I called off the search. I got a can of beer and closed my cabin door—it would dull the screams I would inevitably hear when some neighbor awakened to find a full-grown bullfrog sitting on her chest. A half hour passed, maybe an hour. I sat looking out at the stratified darkness of the American West. Then I heard, *hu-RHUMP*.

The frog was at my feet. I reached to grab him, but he loped away in a series of very fast jumps. I observed that there was no distance at all to the jumps. When I finally caught him, I said, "You bastard, a snake could outjump you!"

As always, the frog was stoic to the point of indifference—which, in truth, made him an otherwise ideal companion for train travel.

We left the train for a few days in Arizona (Amtrak allows one extended layover and reboarding during the course of the trip) because, after enduring a fast passage through the extraordinary scenery of New Mexico, I just couldn't resist anymore. I had to get out and get the feel of the deserts and the hills. The frog, of course, went with me and, while I can't say for certain he appreciated Arizona, I know I did.

2

How I happened to end up pioneering the vortices of the New Aquarian Age and crystal geomantic healing, plus signing, to boot, a petition urging our bastard government to finally release documents that substantiate the existence of extraterrestrial visitors can, I believe, be blamed entirely on the peculiarities of Sedona, Arizona.

It certainly wasn't my fault—nor my intention. And I won't hear a word against my traveling companion, either.

These peculiarities (Sedona's, I mean) were initially described to me at random times and by a variety of people who sat around in the observation car and prattled on and on about the scenery and oddities of the regions through which we passed.

Somewhere near New Orleans a nice lady named Winifred had first mentioned Sedona. She said it was a strange and splendid town; the place she had been united with the many quartz shards she wore on her wrists and around her neck. "Crystals," she called them, and took the time to explain their significance. They help focus my aura," she told me. "They are my conduit to the cosmic source. It has to do with our physical bodies being tuned to the electromagnetic field of the Earth. You know about that, of course?"

I didn't, but I felt obligated to listen.

"Like human radios," Winifred explained. "The Earth constantly transmits an electromagnetic signal—that's why many people feel more at home outdoors than indoors. And because these crystals are from Sedona, they produce much stronger vibrations because Sedona is a power spot; a focal point for the Earth's electromagnetic energies. Not a different frequency, just stronger."

The same voltage, but a stronger amperage, I suggested—as a farm boy, I had been zapped many times by cattle prods and electric fencing, so was intimately familiar with the distinction.

Winifred was delighted with my analogy; said she had never heard the complexities of Sedona grasped so quickly. "That kind of quick insight isn't commonplace," she said. "You really must visit Sedona—I think my crystals are already having an effect on you."

Unlikely but, just to be safe, I avoided Winifred for the rest of the trip. But then I met Mr. Danby, a gray-haired gentleman in a baggy brown suit who, one night in the observation car, eased down beside me, straightened his rope tie, and asked, "You made any sightings, yet?"—an odd question, normally, but we were just west of Alpine, Texas, entering an expanse of desert where, for many decades, lights of an unknown source have been seen but never explained—the Marfa Ghost lights, they are called.

I had been looking for the lights, true, but instead of answering the man, I only shrugged my shoulders and said, "Sightings?"

That was all the encouragement Mr. Danby needed. "Unidentified flying objects," he replied. "The Amtrak tour pamphlet has it all wrong. People have been seeing strange lights in this desert for a hundred years, but they aren't ghosts, they're UFOs—it's those blasted extra-terrestrials! They terrorize west Texas, but the government won't do a thing about it. Afraid the citizenry will panic! And if you think it's bad here, you ought to spend a few days in Sedona, Arizona. Heck, the UFOs spotted here are probably lost and just looking for Sedona, because that's where they have to go to recharge their ships with telluric energy. There are two or three sightings on a *slow* night in Sedona, and don't even ask about the number of abductions."

So I didn't ask. But later in the conversation I did mention that I planned to spend a day or two roaming around Arizona—a thing which made Mr. Danby oddly suspicious. "You ever been to Arizona before?" he asked.

"No."

"You have any reason to leave the train there? Business, maybe? Allergies? Got relatives in the Biosphere?"

"No."

Mr. Danby leaned forward and seemed to study me closely. "You ever suffered unaccountable lapses in memory? Ever dreamed of being locked in a capsule with a strange-looking creature?"

Evidently, he could read the truth in my expression, so I tried hastily to explain, "It's because I've been traveling with a frog; he's in my sleeper right now—"

"God almighty!" Mr. Danby exclaimed. "I knew it the moment I laid eyes on you!"

What it was he knew, Mr. Danby wouldn't come right out and say, but it was easy enough to piece together the implications: I wasn't getting off in Arizona voluntarily—the extraterrestrials were directing my movements. I was being called for reinspection, much like a faulty automobile. At least, that's the way I read it.

"Take my advice, son," Mr. Danby said. "Whatever you do, no matter how hard you got to fight it, do not go to Sedona!"

What rational, reasonable human being could ignore such a warning?

In less than twenty-four hours, driving a white rental car, my frog on the front seat beside me, I was crossing that peculiar town's city limits.

Sedona lies on a branch of the Verde River, a stunning region of earth tones and arroyo greens, all backdropped by red rock spires; the stalagmite remnants of geologic cataclysm that, when isolated by morning sunlight, or smudged by darkness, form a Stonehenge perimeter around a town that some recognize as the hub of New Age Geomancy and Holistic Crystal Spiritualism—a thing that meant much to a few, but nothing at all to me or the frog.

To me, Sedona looked like any other affluent Arizona outpost town. Houses, with their red-tile roofs, were new and of a type:

block and stucco or river rock, with lawns displaying a desert tableau of stone and cactus, as neat as Japanese gardens. Aside from being uncommonly pretty, there seemed to be nothing peculiar about it—an observation a gas station attendant I met was quick to confirm: "People come here thinking this is a town of weirdos. It's not. Mostly, it's a friendly, hardworking kind of place."

What is different about Sedona, though, is that a thriving tourist industry has developed around the belief that the town lies on or near ten major "vortices," which are said to be geological anomalies that are the focal points of the Earth's electromagnetic energies. The gas station attendant didn't tell me this—I read it in a book at the New Age Center, which was just down the street from a long line of New Age bookstores, retail crystal fitters, pyramid palaces, and a pink Jeep tour company that offered Healing Ceremonies, Sacred Places Pilgrimages, and maps to Vortex Power Spots.

Even if I wasn't being summoned by extraterrestrials, a town like this was too good to pass up.

I spent what I thought was to be my only full day in Sedona visiting some of the places recommended to me by the New Age Center. I had a "life reading" at the Spiritualist's Fair, where I was told that I had been a medieval monk in a previous life, and that I now had seven guardian spirits looking after me, almost twice the normal number—happy news, considering my lifestyle. I attended a Hopi festival. I listened to Swiss vocalists singing special healing notes, akin (if I heard right) to the microtonal music of extraterrestrials. After all of this, I spent half an hour sitting beneath a copper pyramid, where, if nothing else, I was impressed by the way it sharpened my thirst.

After a pleasant search for beverages, I stopped at a few of the New Age bookstores where, I must admit, I finally did notice something unusual about Sedona: Almost every person I met claimed to be part Indian. It's true. Not that I could discern their genealogy with my eyes, no. I didn't have to because they came right out and told me, and usually very early on in the conversation. I met part Lakotas, part Apaches, part Hopis, nearly all of whom had Nordic features despite their antecedents, except for one who looked Greek. Yet their heritage was readily visible in the sweeping hand gestures they used to describe the powers of the vortices, their quest as spiritual warriors, and also to give directions. It's a kind of Indian sign language—I know from having watched many westerns on television.

"All people in this country are searching for something," one of the bookstore Indians told me.

Who was I to disagree?

My day in Sedona was interesting and enjoyable, but enough was enough, plus I was on a timetable. So I returned to my room at the New Earth Lodge, loaded my backpack and frog into the car, and headed out. But at a gas station at the edge of town something happened that my life reader had not predicted, and the pyramid had not premonished: I encountered Mr. Danby a second time.

Danby had been planning to come to Sedona all along—that's why he was on the train. "UFOs have been my hobby for twenty years," he said to me. "I first learned of all the ET activity in Sedona from the Armstrong newsletter, and I've been coming here ever since."

A Train, America, and a Frog

Meaning the "Armstrong Report," published by Sedona's Virgil Armstrong, whose book, *ETs and UFOs: They Need Us, We Don't Need Them*, is said, by some, to be the definitive account of Sedona's special relationship with visitors from outer space. (I would later talk with Armstrong—an articulate man, who asked me to pass along this warning: "The frenetic energy created by a nation of untethered people invites alien visitors. They could take over at any time!")

Yet I hadn't seen a single ET or a UFO, which is what I told Mr. Danby.

"Then come along with me tomorrow night, and I'll guarantee you'll see one, maybe both—if you're willing to run the risk."

Personal risk, of course, means nothing to me, but staying an extra day would mean that I would have to miss the Calaveras Jumping Frog Contest, which, to be honest, was an increasingly attractive proposition. Here's why: My frog couldn't jump. Oh, he could hop around fast enough if I was chasing him, but he lacked the athlete's gift of explosive power. He didn't have, I had gradually admitted to myself, that championship fiber described by some as "The look of eagles." Matched against those California frogs, he would humiliate both of us and, worse, embarrass our home state of Florida.

Mr. Danby sweetened the offer by adding, "Bring the frog with you. One night on a vortex will change you both. You'll see a UFO, and your frog will be able to jump ten, maybe twenty feet. The ionic energy boost in those places is amazing!"

The next night, carrying the frog in his box, I met Mr. Danby at what locals call the Airport Vortex (because it's right next to the Sedona Airport), where we followed him up a path, then climbed onto a high saddle of sandstone that overlooked the Verde Valley. I should say right here that those of us who have not evolved spiritually—or who didn't have the foresight to buy a map—would never be able to find a vortex on our own because a vortex looks like any other place, just rock and dirt and a few wind-battered bushes.

"It's what's going on beneath us that makes this place a vortex," Mr. Danby said as we sat down to wait. "Underneath these rocks are veins of iron and basalt running through old lava floes. They release electrical energy—the 'corona discharge effect,' it's called—which energizes our physical and psychic abilities, and also attracts ETs because they need the power to recharge their ships. We must sit very quietly and reverently for a few minutes and you'll be able to feel the ions entering your body."

I sat quietly for a time but felt nothing, so I burped open the lid of the frog's box so the ions could get to him. Having grown up in swamps, maybe he was more attuned to the Earth's energy than I.

That quick, the frog hopped past my fingers and escaped. He jumped away in the darkness while I scrambled in pursuit, slapping my hands on the rocks behind him, always a microsecond too late.

I heard Mr. Danby say softly, "I'll be go to hell. He really does have a frog."

Not at that moment I didn't. The animal wasn't strong, true, but he was quick, and he led me on a zigzag chase across the sandstone . . . and then suddenly disappeared. I stood staring dumbly after him until I realized what had happened.

I turned to Danby and yelled, "My frog just jumped off the damn cliff!"

It was true. I went to the edge and looked over the precipice where, twenty feet below, all was dark and still.

I wasn't in the mood for silence or reverence now. I was angry. That frog and I had covered a lot of miles together and I liked him about as much as a person can like a frog—which, granted, isn't all that much. Still, he was a good frog, and he had no pretenses. He was what he was—a thing that is rare, particularly in people during these frenetic times. But now Danby's absurd promises had made a fool of me and gotten my frog smushed.

I grabbed a flashlight and hustled back down the path, then circled around the spire to the area where the frog should have landed. Above me, I could hear Danby yelling something—what, I didn't understand or care—and then he began to shine his light around the base of the precipice. After only maybe five minutes, I located the frog.

He was alive. He sat there blinking in the glare of light. When I reached to catch him, he made a dozen or so spirited hops. The fall hadn't hurt him a bit and, as if to demonstrate, he bolted toward what appeared to be another cliff.

To the frog, I said, "You dumb ass," and then I carried him back up the path where Mr. Danby, not at all excited, told me a UFO had arrived at the moment of my departure. "You didn't see their searchlight?" he asked. "Apparently, the ETs like you. They were trying to help you find your pet."

"Uh-huh," I said. All I wanted to do was get the frog's box, my car, and get back on the road.

"Did you ever think you'd see that frog jump twenty feet—and live?" Danby pressed. "I'm telling you, it's the power of the vortex! The vortex healed that animal, then attracted the extraterrestrials to help you find him."

As I was leaving, Danby told me that things like that happened all the time. "It's what makes the place special," he said.

When we reboarded Amtrak's *Sunset Limited* late Friday for the final overnight haul into Los Angeles, it was a little bit like coming home. I changed the frog's towel and gave him a double ration of crickets, before I stowed my own gear and showered. Then I sat back and watched through my window as the darkness of Arizona bloomed into the suburban glare of California. In the morning, the new attendant tapped on my door before dawn so that I would be awake for our entrance into Los Angeles. What I saw was tenement blight of an extent that was numbing, everything marked by the graffiti screams of feral children—but the less said about that, the better.

Nothing impressed the frog, and Los Angeles certainly didn't impress me. After all, we had just seen America.

Road Jaundice in Bangkok
and The Hash House Harriers

A subject that deserves discussion is a peculiar malady that sometimes befalls even hard-core, sleep-with-the-animals-type travelers of which this republic has its proud share. You may recognize some of the symptoms. The traveler's gaze hardens while his posture degenerates. The traveler's hands, normally held at ready for an unexpected handshake, become fists. The traveler's foreign vocabulary, once clumsy but at least varied, shrinks to three tough phrases:

"I don't want rice, I want beer."

"Don't ever touch me there again."

"That better not be yak butter."

The affliction has no name, but it should. Travel Rot or Dorothy Syndrome (there's no place like home) would be okay. Road Jaundice might be better, for it accurately describes a kind of yellowing of the spirit that the afflicted traveler experiences. For reasons I don't understand, Road Jaundice usually strikes late in the first week of a trip or early in the third week, and it's a little like having a bad reaction to prescription drugs and being homesick at the same time. To the infected traveler, food that once seemed exotic becomes a foul depot of mired flies and suspicious meats. The native language, which once resembled a warbling flute, becomes a deafening chorus of barking frogs. Ugly business, no doubt, and in the old days a traveler had no choice but to tough it out; to wait for these doldrums to ebb.

Not anymore, though; not for me, anyway. Here is how I stumbled onto a cure:

Several years ago, I was in Medan, Sumatra, which, to a Westerner, is about as bizarre a place as the mind can imagine, what with its lunatic motorized rickshaw traffic, wailing calls to the mosque and wok-fried dog fritters. Spend a couple of weeks there, and you will not wonder why no civic-minded metropolis on Earth would consider choosing Medan as a sister city (the possible exception is Phnom Penh, Cambodia, where opium smokers and sexual deviants still have some say). I had been in Sumatra a lot longer than I wanted, but not nearly as long as I had agreed to stay, so I was wandering the streets, lost as usual, and enduring a grumpy bout of Road Jaundice when I sought refuge in the Pardede Hotel bar. It was there I fell in with a group of Australians who invited me to a ten kilometer jog; what they called a "Hash Run."

But if we ran in this weird country, I wanted to know, might not the police assume we were fleeing some outrageous crime and open fire?

No worries, the Aussies insisted, the running group (The Medan Hash House Harriers they called it) had a long and interesting history on the island and were well known in all quarters.

For reasons you will soon understand, I don't remember a lot of what went on at my first Hash Run. It was in a rural area southwest of Medan, I remember that. The Australians were there, of course, as were men and women from the Netherlands, England, several Asian countries, Scandinavia, and probably some other places, too—about thirty people in all. We stood around talking, getting to know one another (it's a fine thing to hear English spoken while in the grips of Road Jaundice) when, suddenly, someone blew on a horn, yelled "On! On!" and everyone started running at once. Not down the road, mind you, but straight cross-country. We ran up hills, through a pasture, scattered a bunch of ducks in someone's yard, crashed our way through a pretty chunk of jungle, and, just when I'd decided I couldn't go much farther at such a pace, the front runners stopped and began to hunt around in the grass. "Looking for the scent," I was told, which, I later learned, meant they were looking for a paper trail that a pair of runners had laid ten minutes earlier.

About the time I'd caught my breath, someone yelled "On! On!" again, and off we ran once more. And that's the way it went for an hour or more. We'd run through jungle, wade creeks, lope down hills enjoying glorious off-road scenery until the front runners lost the trail, or took a false trail, and then we'd all split up for a bit to search out the correct path. It was like no run I'd ever done before; certainly it was a lot more interesting, and not just because of the bizarre route. My fellow runners seemed to talk in code. "Checking!" they would yell. "On back!" "Slow the bloody FRBs!" (Slow the front running bastards). And: "No passing! You've won yourself a down-down when we get back to the piss bucket." (Translation: Because you're being competitive, you must chug a beverage when we get back to the beer cooler.)

Not that only competitive-type runners had to chug beverages at the conclusion of this Hash House run; nope. The members formed a circle, sang bawdy songs, then contrived outlandish reasons why participants had to do down-downs (chug a beer, or a soft drink), the remainder of which was poured over the drinker's head.

It sounds silly—well, hell, it was silly. No, it was running lunacy. But it was fun. I spent my time in the circle. I spent plenty of time around the piss bucket outside the circle, too. As I said, I don't clearly remember everything that happened at my first Hash House run, but I do remember this: By the time the event was finished, I'd made several new friends, I'd learned a couple of memorable songs, I had a nifty new running T-shirt, and Sumatra didn't seem to be such a foreign place after all. As to my symptoms of Road Jaundice, they were not only temporarily forgotten, they were completely gone.

In short, The Hash House Harriers is an organization that attracts an interesting variety of expatriates and wandering souls who believe that running is a good thing (particularly when it's not done on some prissy road) but socializing afterward is a great thing. Imagine a group of sorority/fraternity travel warriors who have a fetish for bushwhacking and beer drinking, and you'll get a pretty good picture of what hashing is all about.

Not that you have to enjoy alcohol to have fun on a hash run. It not only isn't required, it is never pressed. But if you do enjoy a tankard or two after a butt-busting cross-country jog, you will not lack for companionship.

The best thing about hashing, though, is that visitors are always welcome. It doesn't matter where you're from, who you are, male or female, or how old or young you are. As it says in the organization's guidelines to membership: "No matter what colour, nationality or disability." [As long as it is] Somebody who can take a joke. Someone who doesn't think he is better than any other. Someone not a know-all, arsehole. . . . Someone who is not punch happy, can sit on ice, jump on trains, buses, horse floats . . . and drink out of a running shoe.

In other words, the organization has standards, just not very high standards.

What I didn't know when I stumbled upon The Medan Hash House Harriers is that the organization is worldwide. It has more than 16,000 members attached to 1,191 clubs in 138 countries, and those countries include every far-flung, godforsaken spot on the planet. Stranded in the Sultanate of Oman? There are seven Hash House Harrier clubs around the Oman, and most of them run once a week, year-round. Missed your connections in Mombasa? There The HHH runs every Saturday and Monday. Suffer a case of Road Jaundice in Tonga, Tunisia, or Turkey, Andorra, Argentina, or Algeria, Libya or Palau, Guyana, the Falklands, or Saipan and the cure is only a hash run away. There is an Antarctic HHH, though the runs are seasonal, not weekly, and there are chapters aboard ships at sea, such as England's HMS *Edinburgh* and Australia's HMAS *Stalwart*.

All you have to do to participate is show up. Indeed, some-times The Harriers will send a car (or a rickshaw) to pick you up at your hotel, then drop you back later.

I know a little bit of this from experience, but mostly I'm tak-ing it from The Harrier International World Hash Handbook, which lists pertinent data for every HHH chapter. I consider the handbook a mainstay piece of travel equipage, and I pack it right along with other necessities like clean socks and Lomotil pills. The editor of the book is Tim "Magic" Hughes (for reasons I still don't understand, all Hashers must have nicknames) who also edits *Harrier International* magazine, an irregular periodical for Hash enthusiasts. Hughes, who is the organization's historian and recordkeeper as well, does all of this work on a voluntary breakeven basis using the offices of his Bangkok, Thailand, advertising company as a base for what now must be the largest, strangest, funnest running club in the world.

Recently I was in Bangkok and met with Hughes, who dis-cussed the history and aims of The Hash House Harriers with the same sense of tongue-in-cheek fun that pervades an HHH run. "Running the hash got its start in 1938 in Kuala Lumpur at a colonial establishment known as Selangor Club," Hughes, a Brit who came to Thailand in 1969, told me. "The club had cham-bers set behind it where the bachelors of the day had their billet. The barrack served meals, of course, and became known to its members as The Hash House. One day the members had a run styled after the old hare and hounds paper chase game that was once played in England, and the run was a great success. Back at the Selangor Club, after several rounds of rum drinks, the man who founded the club, A. S. Gispert, proposed the name Hash

House Harriers. It became very popular among the expats of the region."

The second club, according to Hughes, was founded in southern Italy in 1947 by an ex–prisoner of war who had enjoyed some of the Kuala Lumpur runs. The third club was founded in Singapore in 1962 by an Englishman who posted an ad inviting expatriates for a "run and drinks." Although the Hashing clubs became well known in colonial circles, it wasn't until the 1970s that they began to attract a growing number of world travelers and international businesspeople who were impressed by the organization's aims (to promote physical fitness among its members and to get rid of weekend hangovers), and charmed by some of its prohibitions (gaming and opium smoking at the meets are prohibited and the funds of the society shall not be used to pay the fines of members who have been convicted in court).

According to Hughes, the first world hash run—called the InterHash Unconvention—was held in Hong Kong in 1978 hosted by the Kowloon Hash House Harriers. Since then, the week-long celebration has been held every two years in places like Kuala Lumpur, Jakarta, and Sydney, attracting thousands of members from around the world. Recently, InterHash was held in Phuket, Thailand ("Run till you Phuket!"), and, yes, nonmembers were invited.

Hughes told me that the reason he is so passionate about his hobby is that it interweaves so many threads of his own personal interest: history, travel, running, and the outdoors. "Something else I find attractive," he added, "is that the typical Hasher is so irreverent in regard to world events. Hashers run anywhere, anytime, regardless of what is going on around them. For instance, the Kuwait Hash House Harriers had a good turnout for their run on the fourth of August, 1990—which, if you remember, was two days after the Iraqi invasion. They had to wear gas masks because of all that unfortunate smoke from explosions, and several of them were detained by the Iraqis, who were so irritated by their behavior that they smashed the wind screen of the club's car.

"The Himalayan Hash House Harriers," Hughes continued, "held an event at twelve thousand feet near the Tibet border in which the objective was to jog around a sacred lake. Fortunately, though, it was snowing, so they never found the lake—which probably saved them from being shot at by border guards.

"That is one of the grand traditions of the club," Hughes said, "to keep right on running. It goes back to the days of the founding club at Kuala Lumpur, where members continued to hash right through the outbreak of war in 1939. In some book, a British officer tells of setting his men in ambush position in the jungle, waiting for the approaching enemy when, hang it, if fifteen chaps in vests and running shorts from the local harriers club didn't come running past."

Members of the early Hash House club also served very bravely in that war, according to Hughes. "Gispert was killed early in 1942 while defending his post on Bukit Timah," he explained. "His orders had been to detain the Japanese advance as long as possible."

It is precisely this mad-dogs-and-Englishmen persona that makes running with Hashers so much fun. Why exposure to the eccentricities of such a group should void one's impatience with the oddities of a foreign land, I don't know. But it does. And those of us who have suffered Road Jaundice don't much care why.

Croc Poachers of Panama

When it comes to eco ethics, I take a rear seat to no one—certainly not to reptile poachers. But Panama challenges ethics as naturally as it dismantles virtue, so, morally speaking, folding like a cheap tent not only is acceptable, it's a tradition. Even in these days after Manuel Noriega.

Panama is as fun as it is beautiful, no matter who's in charge, and all the invasions in the world aren't going to change that. The country's possibilities are varied and often strange. One minute you're roaming the streets of Panama City, hunting for Pepto-Bismol, the next minute you're in a dugout canoe with two strangers hunting crocodiles. It can happen. It happened to me.

On a Friday morning in Panama City, I purchased a small meat dish from a street vendor. The meat dish was still with me Friday afternoon, gurgling like an eighth-grade science project. It wasn't serious, nothing that required dipping into my drug reserve of Lomotil or Septra, but I still wanted some relief. Plus, I like Central American pharmacies. They're stimulating. They keep you on your toes, for one never knows what chemicals one will walk out with.

Typically, customers file up to a window and hand the pharmacist their needs written on a piece of paper—any paper will do, it doesn't have to be a prescription. Then the customer flies to a neighboring window, where he is given some medicine that has been wrapped in butcher's paper or sealed into a plastic vial. If the customer's Spanish is good, it's probably the medicine he wants. But if the customer's Spanish isn't good, the results can be interesting. Once I asked for time-released cold tablets and left with birth control pills instead. When I tried to exchange the pills, the pharmacist smiled diplomatically and passed me a brown paper sack. There were condoms in the sack. Communication became increasingly confused. So did the pharmacist. So did the people waiting in line behind me, most of whom seemed unconvinced that I needed a condom for every hour of the day.

But finding Pepto-Bismol was no challenge. I walked from my hotel past the Papal Nunciatura where Noriega took refuge during the U.S. invasion, and turned east along shop fronts where security guards idled in the shadows, their automatic weapons slung like guitars. These omnipresent security guards were the only symptoms of unrest in Panama, which came as a surprise because I had been following U.S. newspaper and magazine stories about the country. They had painted a lurid picture of a crime-crazed nation teetering on the ledge of anarchy; a place where all Americans were despised. Instead, I found a lively city nearly unmarked by the recent war, where people were unfailingly friendly. Indeed, recognizing me as an American, Panamanians often introduced themselves on the streets and wished me a pleasant stay.

As a result of the bad publicity, many Panamanians go way out of their way to be kind to visitors, particularly American visitors. Which is why I wasn't surprised, upon perusing the shelves of a nearby *farmacia*, to hear a pleasant voice behind me say, "If you got the craps, it's not the Panamanian water. They got good water here. But if you've got a hangover, it could be the Panamanian beer."

The man, whom I will call Ben, was an American expatriate in his late sixties who said he had come to Panama when life in Louisiana became too tame. "'Bout twenty years ago," he said, "and I wished I'd come about two wives and one prostate operation before that." Ben was in the *farmacia* with his partner Angel, a grinning Panamanian man. The T-shirt I was wearing had rallied their attention: Save The American Crocodile, Skin A Developer.

"Say—you really like crocodiles?" Ben wanted to know. Angel wanted to know, too, judging by the enthusiastic look on his face.

Sure, I told them. It wasn't my T-shirt—I'd borrowed it from a friend and had no plans of giving it back. But I liked crocs well enough, and I was alone in the city and happy for the conversation.

Coincidentally, we moved off down the same aisle (they needed duct tape and bug spray) so the conversation continued.

Would I like to see some crocodiles? Some Panamanian crocodiles?

At first I thought they meant they could recommend a local zoo, but then I saw by their expressions that they meant something else. What, I wasn't sure, though Ben's questions, "You're not too sick to travel a little? You feel okay to do a little work? Can you *swim*?" piqued my interest.

Outside, they told me: The two of them were headed for a river about two hours' drive, and they could use another hand because they were going to catch crocodiles. The guy who was supposed to help hadn't shown. "Catch the crocs alive," Ben said. "Small ones. Tape their mouths and put them in the back of the truck, that simple. It'll take most the night."

It is always unwise to accept invitations from strangers, especially in a foreign land—and why I do it so regularly is anybody's guess. But what were the alternatives? Sit alone in my hotel room, listening to my stomach gurgle? Hang out in the hotel bar watching the U.S. pilots in their flight suits, faces still flushed from crossing the Caribbean at Mach II? I hate being alone in a hotel room, and I hate hotel bars, and exchanging these two bleak options for a night on a jungle river seemed worth the risk.

I squeezed into the truck cab with Ben and Angel—Angel drove—and we were nearly an hour out of Panama City before I knew for sure that I had fallen in with poachers. Before leaving, Ben had assured me that Angel had a government permit for taking twenty crocs. They seemed proud of the permit, for they said they were going to sell to a nearby reptile farm that was strict about buying only legally captured animals.

"They're all strict these days," Ben said. "Everything's gotta be tagged. Everything's gotta have a permit. Even in Panama. Never thought I'd see the damn day."

I wouldn't have become suspicious, but the permit was mentioned so often that it clearly was a novelty—they were used to doing this work without permits, and now they were enjoying a night of respectability. Or were they? I wasn't so sure when I learned how fate and good fortune had brought the permit into Angel's hand.

"One thing about wars," Ben told me, "they tend to cause a lot of confusion."

I could only agree and wait for him to explain.

We were driving northwest on a lean asphalt trail that seemed to be guided by the jungle that dominated it; a great green presence, cool to the nose, that steered the highway through partitions of light and gloom; sheer walls of vine spotted with bright bursts of color: butterflies and iridescent blooms, and then fireflies as it got darker. I rode along, arm out the window, listening.

Finally, Ben said, "Another thing about wars is, government workers won't go anywhere near their buildings. If there's no war, you can't pry the lazy bastards out of their offices with a crowbar. But start dropping a few bombs, and they scurry. 'Fraid they're gonna get blowed up."

"Sí, true, true," agreed Angel, grinning, always grinning. "I go looking for a permit at the very bad time. Right during the war, but nobody in the permit office. They all hiding. So I give myself the permit. It's legal. I signed it myself."

Ben looked on in admiration. "Choppers flying all over the place looking for Noriega, but it was business as usual for ol' Angel there. He went into the municipal building looking for opportunity, and he come out with that permit for twenty crocs, plus a certificate that says he's a state-bonded plumber, and picked himself out a chauffeur's license to boot." Ben leaned across me to say to Angel, "And you don't even own a car. You shoulda got a liquor license! We could have done something with that. Wars don't happen along every day."

Thieves, I thought to myself. *Poachers and thieves*.

Ben leaned back and added, "But it's like I always say: If a person can't profit from adversity, he damn well deserves to suffer."

Suffering is a condition inevitably shared by all indigenous creatures, human and otherwise. The shape of the pyramid is well established, the lines of injury long ago formed. Just as all the invasions in the world won't diminish the beauty of Panama, all the Earth Days and hip eco cartoons in the world won't dent a more compelling reality: To a community of hungry people, wildlife isn't a resource, it is table fare. To a community of poor, wildlife isn't a natural wonder, it is chattel to be eaten or sold. The same with rivers and rainforests. Photos of teary-eyed seals and gnawed rabbit legs aren't going to change that—nor should they be expected to. People have as much right to exist as otters and dolphins, and if the crunch was really on, even the most self-righteous would elbow their way toward the killing fields. No one can argue that American groups now so passionate about animal rights are dominated by descendants of the same affluent class who pushed wading birds to extinction because they fancied egret feathers in their Sunday hats; a group that once generated the same faddish enthusiasm for raccoon coats and safari shoots that members now display at Save the Whale rallies.

To people surviving on the precipice, criticism from the terminally trendy carries little validity and less weight. Modern times create modern ironies. Fifty years ago, "backward" nations were characterized by a dearth of industry but a wealth of natural resources. Today, many of those same nations have nibbled those assets to the nub; have sold their future piecemeal with as little foresight as stray dogs pissing on fire hydrants. In some places, now the crunch really is on.

On a trip through the rainforests of Sumatra, I was astonished by the realization that some of the most remote jungle rivers in the world had almost no fish, and one of size. Zero. America's worst industrial rivers supported more life. The river fisheries had withstood a thousand generations of netting, but they could not survive the combined assault of car batteries and hand-crank telephones that local people used to shock the fish, or the poisons locals used to stun them—nor the suffocating turbidity created by clear-cut logging. Confronted by such techniques, the fish were as helpless as rhinos and African elephants sprinting from machine guns.

The destructive—and just plain addle-brained—behavior of driven people is tragic enough, but when profiteering is added to the equation, the straits become desperate. But with all the new regulations worldwide and the manpower devoted to enforcement, it's getting tougher to make a living as a poacher.

Ben had said that—it's getting tougher. Which was why he and Angel were so pleased with the permit to capture and keep twenty American crocodiles (*Crocodylus acutus*), which is now one of the rarest reptiles in the Americas.

"You shoulda got a permit for a hundred," Ben said more than once. "This river where we're going, I can get you a hundred.

Two hundred if you want. I haven't been there for about ten years, so they should be thick."

Prior to my visit, when I thought of Panama, I pictured the canal and the military bases, and not much else. I did not expect to find a biological wonder; a rich land of rainforest and jungle and remote rivers. But that's what Panama is. Ironically, though, Costa Rica and Belize attract far more tourists—which is good for those of us who prefer to make our own paths. In Panama, you can make a path easily enough once away from the city.

"Wait 'til you see this river," Ben kept telling me. "If you like wild places, you're going to love this river."

After more than two hours of driving, Angel turned onto a dirt road, past some concrete block houses, past some bamboo huts with thatched roofs, and Ben directed him to a clearing where he said a friend had hidden a boat for them.

The moon was up now, the night was clear with stars, and we found the boat in the moonlight, a long open chalupa, or dugout canoe, with a motor. We had to push and carry the boat more than a hundred yards from the road to the river, which is why they had recruited a stranger to help—the thing must have weighed four hundred pounds, and neither Ben nor Angel were young men.

"That was a regular hemorrhoid tester," Ben hooted when we finally got the water. "Bastard's heavier than it was fifteen years ago, huh, Angel?"

Maybe so, but Angel was still grinning. And he kept grinning while he and I wrestled the hand-hewn hulk into the water.

Mosquitoes had found me, I was soaked with sweat—and Ben wasn't far wrong in his assessment regarding hemorrhoids. Even so, it was a pretty place. A nice night to be out. The river was a gray void in the moonlight, a narrow clearing that evaporated into the forest gloom. I could smell the rot of hardwood leaves, but there was a hint of mangrove, too; an odor of salt and sulfur, and I knew we were not far from the sea.

Ben steered. I sat on the wet floor in the middle of the chalupa and Angel took the bow, holding a long pole with a rope noose at the end. Ben had a spotlight, and he shined it high into the trees to preserve his night vision as we ran. The beam of light was like a column of yellow vapor through which giant moths and bats darted. Over the noise of the engine, Ben promised we'd see our first croc around the next bend, and he swung the light down to the river bank. There was a pair of amber eyes, but it was a mammal, not a reptile.

"Gato negro," Angel said over his shoulder. Black cat. But it wasn't a cat, it was a martenlike animal I had never seen before. Ben followed it with the spotlight as it twisted off into the bushes.

"There'll be a croc around the next bend," Ben promised again.

But there wasn't. Nor did we find one in the next hour. But we found several sloths. We saw four or five peccaries. We saw more bats, and there was a moth that, with its wings open, looked just like the face of an owl.

"Someone musta hunted this place since the last time I was here," Ben admitted finally. "Cleaned the place out." But he knew a branch, he said, where there would certainly be crocs. "We got a permit," he reminded us. "And we got all night."

An Island Off Borneo

Sipadan Island, Sabah, Borneo—a side benefit of exotic dive travel is that you acquire bits of language not normally heard in the hurly-burly of modern commerce and, so, are guaranteed to impress the folks at home. Some examples from my marathon journey to this tiny island east of Sumatra, west of New Guinea, located at the very back of beyond: *Penyu* (turtle); *Ajaib* (magic); *Pelajan paheyin tambar bir.* (Waiter, we require more beer.); *Air biru* (Blue water); *Pulau* (Island); *My ke put koo!* (Drop that blowgun!).

Depending on how far you go, and the length of time you stay, even a list of non sequiturs like this can become useful; indeed, can exert a kind of karmic influence, adding shape and fabric to a trip. On Sipadan, the synthesis began with my first dive.

A stone's throw from my thatch-roofed cottage, the sea bottom drops abruptly to 240 feet. Another stone's throw, it sheers nearly half a mile. Drifting down that coral wall was more like soaring than descending. Sipadan is a jungled apex; less than thirty acres breach the surface. The mountain lies below where, weightless, I floated over bluffs and crags, down the parapet reef. There were clown trigger fish, anthius goldfish, velvet-hued unicorns, and hundreds of other species I did not recognize. The coral walls might have been a Disney garden; the fish might have been wild flowers or butterflies. If you dive, you know the protoplasmic gush and flow of activity. You know the streaming colors. The individual elements blur into a single glittering pointillist painting. You might be in the Celebes Sea, but you might also be in the Caribbean, or the South Pacific—or at some Sea World venue. The effect is overwhelming. It numbs.

But then I saw my first sea turtle; a huge green turtle flapping out of the murk. The animal was as big as me; it had to weigh more than two hundred pounds. Its carapace was olive hued and fouled with benthic travelers. The stroke of its flippers mimicked the wing stroke of seabirds; barnacles on its shell mimicked the shapes of spent volcanoes.

I saw another . . . and another. There were sea turtles everywhere. They floated above me, they were silhouettes on the edge of visibility. There were turtles grazing on the patina of living corals; turtles wedged into crevices as I drifted along, their reptilian eyes dark and indifferent.

It was on my first dive, on the high reaches of the abyss, that I thought of a more appropriate name for Sipadan. *Pulau Penyu:* Island of Turtles.

Back on the beach, I ordered *bir*. The sea was *air biru*, without a horizon. I sat on the dock and watched the big greens surface. When their dinosaur heads punched through the sea membrane, they opened their beaks and hissed.

The island was showing itself, drawing meaning from my strange word list.

The island was *ajaib*.

Some dive spots, getting there is half the fun. Some dive spots, getting there is none of the fun. Sipadan is a little of one and a lot of the other. After forty-two hours in airports and on planes, after a seven-hour layover in Kuala Lumpur, after a lunatic bus ride from Tawau to Semporna, and after surviving an open boat crossing of the Mabul Passage in which, for the first time in my life—*the first time in my life*—I voluntarily put on a life jacket, I think I can say that.

In the sometimes snooty game of exotic diving, degree of difficulty matters. Sipadan ranks right up there.

At the docks in Semporna, my shaving kit and I (my luggage hasn't been seen since we left Florida) set off on Borneo Diver's twenty-eight-foot transport, through the straits of the Celebes Sea, bound for Sipadan, eighteen miles away. The sea coast of southeastern Borneo is lovely: jungle fringe, shoal water villages of zinc-roofed stilt houses, gold-domed mosques, candy-colored longboats under sail—all but unknown to tourists until the mid-1980s when Jacques Cousteau's film crew discovered Sipadan ("We have found an untouched piece of art!") and the rush of sport divers began. After so many hours in the air, and after the terrifying ride from Tawau, it was wonderful to climb into an open boat. A person can breathe on an open boat; he can relax a little, for the chances of experiencing a sudden loss of cabin pressure, or of colliding with a lumber truck are practically nil. But my sense of well-being didn't last. We made our way toward Ligitan Channel, past the fishing kampongs of Bum Bum Island, then, leaving Hood Hill and its cascade of forest in our wake, we dolphined toward the open water of Mabul Passage.

My helmsman was Omar Kamar, a Borneo Diver's staff and, presumably, a veteran of hundreds of crossings, so I was unconcerned by the freshening wind and the squall curtain drifting toward us. In an open boat, one expects to get wet; indeed, after four days in the same clothes, I craved a good hosing. Even when the seas convoked an ugly cross-chop, swelling into open ocean rollers, I wasn't worried. But then we took a wave over the bow . . . and another . . . then Omar let out a guttural *whoop* just before a really monstrous wave tipped us skyward, swinging our craft beam to the sea. Another wave hit us, flooding out one of the two outboard motors, and, for a sickening few seconds, I thought we were going to capsize. Equipment was careening around the boat's interior; something fell from the canvas canopy and whacked me on the head—a life jacket!

One doesn't quibble with providence; God knows His business. I strapped the jacket on while exhorting Omar to buckle down and get that starboard engine going, or our bloated bodies wouldn't be found until they surfed to shore in New Guinea.

Omar got the engine started. We banged along. Within the hour, Sipadan Island slowly assembled form on the horizon: a high hardwood interior fringed by coconut palms and beach. There was a dock, guest cottages built on stilts, and boats suspended along an abrupt color demarcation, violet water banded to a nucleus of bronze, that showed the island for what it is: a sea pinnacle that rises from the belly of the abyss.

Fourteen thousand miles, luggage lost, almost swamped at sea, but, when asked about this trip, the first words out of my mouth will be: "You wouldn't believe the turtles."

This says something about Sipadan.

It says something about diving.

My dive buddy has accompanied me from the States; a cardiac surgeon who, upon hearing that I was off to Borneo, insisted, "Those tropical climes can be murderous. You'll require a personal physician." For the record, though, he is the only one who has suffered any physical indisposition on this trip. I suspect he got ahold of some bad bean curd in Kota Kinabalu because, at night, his stomach gurgles like fermenting yeast. Otherwise, he is an ideal partner, for our approach to the sport is similar. SCUBA divers come from all walks of life, span demographics, yet they can still be divided into two broad groups. There are divers who are dedicated students of the craft. They read the journals, they keep detailed logs. If they don't own the latest high-tech equipage—Veloce fins, Kevlar BC vests, air-integrated dive computers, PolarTech wet suits, Amphibico video housings—they would like to, and probably will. New and exotic dive places are a passion; they race from hot spot to hot spot. T-shirts from places like Palau, the Great Barrier Reef, and the Solomon Islands are considered badges of conquest and a measure of their own proficiency. These people are the best of the sport; the aficionados of SCUBA.

The second type of diver is less attractive in every way. Their enthusiasm for SCUBA may have flamed brightly for a while but, for reasons known only to them, it waned, so now, if they dive at all, it is supplemental to what they consider more interesting objectives, or when there's nothing else to do. They covet little, they study less. These people are dabblers; they are the sport's dilettantes.

Of the two groups, my partner and I would prefer to be associated with the former but, in fact, are archetypes of the latter—a truth I would like to keep hidden from our fellow divers, but the odds aren't good. For one thing, I am the only diver on the island who doesn't have a wet suit. I've been blaming it on my lost luggage, but if my bag ever does arrive, my underwater apparel won't much change: running shorts, T-shirt, and a bandana to keep my head warm. True, in Sipadan's eighty-degree water, I'm perfectly comfortable, but I am also painfully aware that, en route to dive sites, everyone else appears dressed for space flight while I look as if I'm headed for gym class. In SCUBA, as in skiing, style points count, and I am running up a big deficit on this little island.

Also, discourse with the other guests is telling. There are, perhaps, forty other divers at the Borneo facility, and I have already met most of them (interaction with guests at the other two lodges is discouraged). The informal meeting place is the dining lodge, where, beneath ceiling fans and a thatch ceiling, divers sit around munching snacks and trading stories until it is time to go back into the water again. In principle, SCUBA diving is not a competitive sport but, in practice, it often is; a competition that takes place ashore in the thrust and parry of conversation, the objective of which is to establish one's superior expertise. Not that I met many SCUBA snobs on Sipadan. Indeed, one of the island's most attractive features was the near absence of these obnoxious goofs (perhaps they are territorial; found only on the Florida Keys or Caribbean dive resorts). But with the few we met, my dive partner and I didn't fare well.

Them: "So what kind of computer are you recommending to novices these days?"

Partner: "Uh . . . hum . . . well, I defer to Randy on those matters. I'm a surgeon, you understand—"

Me: "Computer? Uh . . . Macintosh has got a little clicker, so you don't even have to read the directions—"

Them: "*Dive* computer."

Me: "Oh! Ah! Well, opinions vary. Yes. There are so many on the market now. Not like the old days."

Them: "That's certainly true!"

Me: "But . . . generally speaking, I recommend the waterproof variety. Yes, I strongly recommend that."

We do better in the game of geographical name dropping for, while we are SCUBA dilettantes, we are at least well-traveled dilettantes, so can assemble quite a list. My partner has dived the Keys, the Caymans, and Cay Sal, and I have dived such interesting and esoteric places as Central America, Isle of Pines, Cuba, Ningaloo Reef and Shark Bay, Western Australia, Fiji, and Tahiti—if you count skin diving, which I do and to great effect.

But, as I said, we haven't had to spend much time in this verbal fencing, for most of the people here are as unaffected as the surroundings. To name a few, we have met Walda from Saudi Arabia, Careen from the Netherlands, Christine from

Switzerland, Bert and Mary from Shanghai via Kenya, Kevin from Oxford, Peter and Michelle from Nurnberg, and Peggy and Gary from Oregon.

SCUBA divers get around. As Walda told me, "It's an international language."

Sometimes an exotic dive hot spot is like a fishing hot spot, or a secret ski run. Because conditions vary, people are quick to say, "You should have been there yesterday."

Today's dives included West Ridge, South Point, and White Tip Avenue where, a joke circulating around the lodge says, there is no avenue and there are no sharks.

Not entirely true judging from my recent experience, but it's close.

Located off the eastern shore of the island, the site called White Tip Avenue is only five minutes away by boat. There we followed Ahmad down to eighty feet, then drifted the wall, gradually ascending during the next hour to surface level. During the course of the dive, visibility deteriorated from sixty feet to less than thirty feet, so the murky water may have been the reason we saw so few fish. I saw one small white tip shark, but he spooked at our approach, and only two or three snapper and grouper of size. There was a plethora of small tropicals, however, and lionfish were common—as were sea turtles, of course.

West Ridge wasn't any better but, at South Point, visibility was a consistent fifty to sixty feet and there, along with the many turtles, were hundreds of big jacks in a formation so solid that they blocked the sun, their shadows creating an eerie dusk.

Even so, back in the boat, reviews from members of my group were less than enthusiastic. One man said West Ridge would go down as one of the worst dives he had ever logged, and the general feeling of the group was that Sipadan wasn't equal to the glowing accounts they had read in their dive magazines. Not that they hated the place—it was good, just not great. I am less quick to pass judgment not because I doubted the magazine stories (I haven't read them) but because I realize that, *in a wilderness situation, wildlife can't be programmed to perform like some Epcot exhibit.* The ocean has no bars; pelagic fish come and go, visibility changes with the currents. The schools of great hammerheads or the giant manta rays that have been seen and photographed here may have been hanging just beyond the scrim of sight, or they may have preceded us by minutes. Still, it is hard not to join in the speculation that the fish population is reaching to the fourteen-hour dive days and the heavy census of divers on this tiny, tiny island. What I find most disappointing is the paucity of big reef fish, such as snappers and groupers, that are also prized table fare. When I took up SCUBA diving in 1970, schools of food fish that had not been terrorized by spearfishermen could still be found, and I think my interest in the sport faded with them. But Sipadan is a national preserve; fishing is not allowed. So why have I seen so few?

When I questioned one of the staff, he said, "You should have been here last month. And last year was even better!"

On Sipadan, life at two atmospheres may be *vagarious* by nature, but life at one atmosphere is, by nature, fun. I like the routine, I love the food, and I am fascinated by the island. We are up at first light and pad barefooted down the beach to breakfast. After the two morning dives, we meet again at the lodge for lunch, dive again around three P.M. Then it's dinnertime, and the food, served family style, is always interesting: fried fish, goat curry, sweet and sour pork, bok choi, mustard greens, native fruits, beef in sate sauce, rice, fried chicken, potatoes, and other good things; a strange and wonderful mixture of food that seems mostly Asian, but with an unexpected dash of the American South. Then we sit around over Tiger beer, exchanging stories, or stroll out onto the dock and watch sea turtles thrash around in the water, copulating in a floundering green spray of biolumin-escence. At bedtime, we retreat to our stilt cottages where the island's generator keeps the ceiling fan whirring and the reading lights bright.

Sometimes, if we don't feel like reading, we stay and have an *irau*—that means "party" in Malay.

All in all, not a bad life, but this afternoon, I broke the routine by skipping the afternoon dive so that I could hike into the jungle interior. It didn't take long (I can jog around the whole island in ten minutes) yet the contrast between the vista of blue and the vista of green was striking and, frankly, a relief after so much time underwater looking at coral. Only a few yards from the beach, the great hardwood trees and vines of rain forest dom-inate. There were strange palms and strangler figs and waist-high ferns. Back on the Borneo mainland, I had been told that, in ear-lier times, fishermen had avoided Sipadan because they believed a giant octopus lived in a sea cavern at the center of the island, its tentacles long enough to wrestle people into its lair—a ridicu-lous story when heard on a city street, but spooky when one is alone in the heart of such a place. But I saw no octopus, only purple-tailed anoles, a few land crabs, and a flock of imperial pigeons.

Naturally, at dinner tonight, members of my group told me I had missed the best dive so far. They had seen a lot of small whitetip sharks and a few barracudas. "But it wasn't great," one man told me. "The visibility was only fair." Not that the mood was gloomy—it never is in the lodge. Bert told wonderful stories about his travels in Africa, Peter lectured on the superiority of Nurnberg beer ("All those chemicals! American beer is poop!"), and Peggy described her life in the Pacific Northwest ("In Oregon, a woman can't be too skinny, too rich, or own too much duct tape").

I don't keep a dive log, but my morning notebook entry reads: "Barracuda point. Best dive of the week. 70' visibility. Dropped down on a school of giant bumphead parrot fish, some to 80 pounds. Then a whole shoal of barracuda; thousands of them, like a curtain of saber blades. Put myself in the middle of them and drifted through. Maybe two dozen whitetip sharks cruised the perimeter. Current so strong that it was similar to being swept along by a mountain river. There were moments when I was out of control; had no hope of stopping myself. Not that I minded."

One of our group minded. He told me later that he had felt we were being pushed out to sea, and that he had almost panicked. I'm glad he confided in me because, truth is, I lied in my note-book. I was scared. Still, it was a great dive. One of my best ever—not that I keep score, though a lot of divers do.

Tonight, some of the divers in the lodge were checking scores and comparing them. Under discussion were the best dive spots in the world, and they hunkered to it. After a lot of beer, and some mild arguments, here are their top five: (1) Maldive Islands, South Pacific. (2) Palau, South Pacific. (3) The Red Sea. (4) The Great Barrier Reef, Australia. (5) Sangalakki, Borneo (just opened to divers, Sangalakki is being called "the new Sipadan").

Human nature being what it is, Sipadan didn't have a shot of breaking into the lineup. It was the only spot everyone had in common, so, even if they felt it was the best, no one would have risked admitting it. Also, there was talk that there are just too many divers in the water to enjoy any sense of isolation. Also, visibility just hasn't been good.

But why worry so much about the visibility? As I told one of the divers, "It's not like we have to land an airplane down there."

In Malay, the phrase *Tidak apa* means "It just doesn't matter."

This business of ranking dive spots is silly. I thought about it this morning as I circumnavigated the island (it took me forty-three minutes), alternately swimming hard, then slowing to peruse the aquarium colors of the shallows. Here's just one example of why it is silly: Last night, after the Best Dives forum, Vasiliki, a beautiful Greek actress, softened the mood when she sat down and sang torch songs accompanied by Ahmad on his guitar. Listening to someone like her sing, with a South China breeze blowing through the palms, is a peerless way to spend an evening. Like Yien, Vasiliki is extremely *menawan*. She's a gifted vocalist, too.

And it got better. Fast Eddie did more card tricks. Then the lodge staff performed, and an impromptu *irau* blossomed and gathered strength. Around ten P.M. I learned a new word and jotted it in my notebook: Mabok. It means "beer happy." Even those who weren't drinking seemed a little *mabok*. We had a fine time.

Later, as my partner weaved his way back to our hut, he observed, "To hell with the diving—this was worth the trip." It was an offhand remark that carried a lot of truth. Diving is essentially a solitary act, and the personal worth of each experience is judged subjectively and privately—if it is judged at all. There are no best spots in the world to dive.

There are only favorite spots.

Pavlov's Hogs

There was much to recommend the rain-forest coast of northeastern Australia, many curios and recreations—giant crocs, coral reefs, and tree-climbing kangaroos among them—but, for the moment, my attention was devoted to the topic at hand, namely, the conditioning of Doctor Pavlov's dogs.

"Fit little dears, what? Hoh! They love to run, the lot of 'em. Especially when they get a pig up their nostrils." When Peter Pavlov, Ph.D., is describing his dogs, "Pig up the nostrils" is a much used expression.

There were four: all of them cattle cur and kelpie crossbreeds, each of them blue glazed with shepherd patching. They had names. Of course they had names. Does it come as a surprise that a man named Pavlov would name his dogs? There was Kazi, the lead dog. Heckle and Meat were scouts. And little Meg, only nine months old, was serving her apprenticeship, learning to hunt. "Not easy up in the bush," Pavlov reminded me. "Dog has to learn about pigs. Just the same as people!"

Pig-dogs and dogging pigs: Pavlov's two favorite subjects. He is, after all, one of Australia's foremost experts on feral hogs; a dedicated field biologist who has spent the last seventeen years researching and writing about the esoterica of wild swine. *Feral Pigs, Ungulate Predators* is one of his monographs. *The Behaviour of Feral Pigs in Flocks of Lambing Ewes* is another. And those who suspect that Pavlov's interest in dogs is selfishly utilitarian would do well to read his *Comparative Dimensions of Testes of Australian Dingoes*. "Fascinating animal, the dingo," Pavlov might tell you. "Did you know that the Australian kelpie was developed by crossing dingoes with British sheepdogs? Study the dingo, then spend a few months in the bush watching my dogs work pigs, you won't doubt it. Oh yes, there are similarities!"

Already I was learning a lot from Doctor Pavlov and I had every reason to believe that arranging a meeting with him was one of the smartest moves I had made since arriving in Queensland. And arranging a meeting wasn't easy. Between Cairns and Mossman I had made general inquiries: Were there any researchers around doing interesting field work? My motivation wasn't scientific, it was selfish—the reasons are complex; I'll explain them later. Even so, I was eager to hook up with some reputable professional who could lead me into the outback, and Pavlov's name was always on the short list. More interestingly, his name was always offered with a strange mix of reticence and amusement: "When it comes to the rainforest, Peter Pavlov's good value. But, believe me, mate, you don't want to go pig shooting with Piggy!"

That's what Pavlov did—hunted pigs and shot them. I am not prissy about such things; it came as no surprise. This, after all, is the white man's way: First kill it, then study it. My enthusiasm grew.

Pavlov was well known in small coastal visages such as Daintree and Wonga. Even small children referred to him as "Piggy." Nearly everyone hinted, implied, or just came right out and told me that only the foolhardy would follow the man into the woods. "You come to Oz on holiday, right, mate? Well, a day in the bush with Piggy Pavlov's no holiday!"

Which is exactly why I traveled up the coast to Cape Tribulation National Park where Pavlov, as well as pursuing his own private research on feral hogs, is also employed as the Cassowary Conservation Officer (the cassowary is a rare emu-size bird with a prehistoric barnaclelike helmet on its head).

I got lucky. Pavlov had been in the field and was just getting ready to go back out again but, yes, he supposed he could stop by the fancy eco lodge where I was staying. "Bit of a chat-up about pigs?" he asked. "Righty-oh. Not a problem. But could we meet in the parking lot? I'll be bringing my dogs, of course, and the lodge's guests might not appreciate four pig dogs splashing around in their pool."

That seemed prudent. The eco lodge had a nice pool. We met in the parking lot.

In appearance, Peter Pavlov is a cheerful, gnomish mix of outdoorsman and academician. He has wild red hair, a prospector's whiskers, and the kind of bandy, bowed legs that I had previously seen only on Gurkha mercenaries and a certain manic type of Outward Bound instructor. Horn-rimmed glasses gave him a bookish look, but the khaki shorts and field cap were pure

Australian. Same with his pattern of speech: Each sentence ended with a gradual upward inflection, from tenor to second soprano, so that when he laced several sentences together it sounded as if he were attempting to sing.

"Am I related to Pavlov the famous researcher? I'm often asked that. Yes, it's not an unfamiliar question to me."

Well. . . . ?

"Oh, it's possible, I suppose. Yes, it is certainly possible."

But it seemed more than possible. It was probable. Nobel laureate Ivan Pavlov was a ruling-class Russian. Piggy Pavlov's father was an anticommunist White Russian who migrated to Australia during the postrevolution chaos just eighteen years after Ivan won the prize. Furthermore, the existence of these dogs bouncing all around the parking lot, lathering Piggy's hands, seemed final affirmation. Is there anyone who really understands the power of genetic memory? But I took it as the best of omens—as well as the mark of Piggy Pavlov's strong character— that he did not fawn over the connection to his famous relative. I have learned not to expect such rectitude from academia's ego-brittle members.

Also, and to be honest, it was difficult to get Pavlov to talk about anything but pigs. And his dogs. And how his dogs dealt with pigs. If those topics lagged, there were dingoes. But pigs were first and foremost on his agenda. Did I know that feral pigs were a terrible environmental problem worldwide? Did I realize that feral pigs not only destroyed the rain forest with their constant rooting, but also impacted on indigenous fauna by hogging the food and, worse, preying on helpless young? Hawaii was a good example. Feral pigs were destroying the islands! Agriculture also suffered. In Pakistan, Asiatic boars competed with rats to destroy crops. In 1977, in New South Wales, feral pigs had almost single-handedly destroyed the wheat harvest. And when it came to sheep, feral pigs were the grimmest of grim reapers.

"I had to go to the African literature to truly understand the behavior of feral pigs," Pavlov told me. We were still in the parking lot. His dogs had yet to find the eco lodge's pool. "Have you ever read about hyenas? Hyenas are one of the few animals that kill for sport. Particularly on rainy, chill nights. 'Thrill kill,' the literature calls it." Pavlov looked at me. "Do you know what other animal kills just to kill?"

I took a guess. "Feral pigs?"

"Exactly! Pigs are predators, never forget it. Oh, they'll knock down a lamb and devour it in the blink of an eye. They are extremely destructive animals and we really must find a way to deal with them." When he said that, his tone illustrated his dislike for feral pigs, but also conveyed an underlying joy that they existed. If not for them, what would he and his dogs hunt?

Piggy talked on about pigs. It was interesting—it truly was. But, in time, I brought the conversation around to the reason for our meeting: Could I join him on one of his field trips?

Surprisingly, Pavlov was reluctant. There wasn't that much to see, he said. Field work was actually rather boring. He hemmed and hawed, the prelude to polite refusal.

I pressed.

It was then that Piggy Pavlov said something that would later haunt me. He said, "People have come along before, mate, and it's never worked out. They just didn't understand that you must have a . . . have a, well . . . a very high tolerance for *inconvenience* to hunt pigs." It was phrased as understatement, of course, but it did not seem a cloak for maliciousness as understatement so often is. No, Piggy Pavlov was cheerful and kind and brilliant, and he remained so. He had stated his objections in a way that left the responsibility and the decision up to me.

I made it.

The next morning at five we left in search of pigs.

I said that my motivation for seeking out a field biologist was selfish, and it's true. From past experience, I knew that traveling with a researcher, just about any researcher, is a good way to see and become familiar with just about any kind of habitat. No matter what their specialty, biologists usually have a solid peripheral understanding of where things are and of who is doing what to whom. It's true that biologists are prone to eccentricity (they spend way too much time alone—difficult because fantasy is the first casualty of scientific training), but I, for one, like eccentrics. Furthermore, it had been my experience that field researchers behaved . . . well, reasonably while in the field. They didn't invite blisters with hard forced marches, they didn't invite injury by making difficult climbs. For them, wilderness was a place of study, not an instrument for measuring their machismo, which is to say that they took a lot of rest stops and often brought interesting things to drink.

So that's one selfish reason I sought out Peter Pavlov. Another is that I had spent nearly two weeks four-wheeling around Northeastern Queensland and I was weary of the constant tourist flow and roadside scenery. Nothing against Northeastern Queensland, mind you. Queensland is Australia's tropical rim; the emerald fringe of the antipodean dust bowl. Twenty miles or less offshore is the Great Barrier Reef, the most spectacular reef system in the world. Between Townsville and Cape York are a thousand miles of Coral Sea beach, much of it veined with rivers and shadowed by mountainous rain forest. This rain forest strand contains more then seven hundred different species of trees as well as animals found nowhere else on the globe.

Northeastern Queensland—Australians call it the Wet Tropics—is gorgeous. As I said, it possesses curios and recreations enough to recommend it. But it is precisely because of this that the region is also Australia's biggest tourism draw. Travelers from the Pacific rim and around the world come to view its wonders. They come by the thousands; by the tens of thousands. The international port of Cairns, like Key West, is a fun coastal town with its own funky sense of history. But Cairns, also like Key West, is on a balls-out tourist binge. Cairns's main strip, The Esplanade, crackles along Trinity Bay with a riot of hand painted "BOOK HERE!" signs so new that the paint barely seems dry. The signs flog ecotourism, car rentals, reef trips, float planes, white water raft excursions, croc trips, hot air balloons, and gourmet food backpacking outfitters, one of which challenged: "ARE YOU FIT ENOUGH?"

This was sufficiently unsavory but, worse, almost all the tours relied on the single road north out of Cairns for access to the rain forest and beaches. Even the brutal four-wheel-drive-only sections above the Bloomfield River crossing were so busy that they resembled a Toyota road rally. No matter where I went along the coast, I couldn't escape the impression that I was in the world's largest theme park; a green and spacious attraction through which the Nikon snapshooters, cruise couples, the washed-out hippie pretenders, yupsters and Greensters alike all chauffeured themselves. It was after about a week of this bullshit that I began to make serious inquiries about field researchers.

But enough of this. I was with Piggy Pavlov and we were hunting feral hogs. And not too successfully at first. While it was still dark, he packed me into his old four-by-four among the chattering dogs and drove to a nearby beach fringe. The fringe was heavily wooded. Pavlov threw open the vehicle's doors and introduced me to his hunting technique: The dogs chased the pigs and we chased the dogs. The initial chase covered a couple of hours and more than a couple of miles. It was pleasant. The woods were fresh with the medicinal odor of eucalyptus trees and rose gum, yet the sea breeze smelled of open ocean. Every now and then Pavlov would hand me his M1 carbine to hold while he ducked through vines or stopped to study hog sign. There was a lot of hog sign. He certainly hadn't exaggerated the damage the pigs were doing. Whole sections of forest had been rooted bare. It looked as if a mad, random bulldozer had been at work. But the dogs didn't corner a single pig.

"Not a problem," Pavlov told me. "Oh, they're smart, pigs are. That's why it takes eighteen months or more to get a dog trained properly. And this is the easy part of my work! I'm not in this for the hunt, understand. It's purely scientific. After we take a pig or two, then we have to do the necropsy. Have to see what they're eating to understand just what they're destroying. And, of course, check the liver parasites. Bloody work, mate. I once had a pig's intestines explode in my beard! Wasn't very pleased about that, I'll tell you!"

We drove to another area—a highland rain forest named Mount Sorrow—and began to hike up hill through dense brush. As we did, Pavlov chatted along happily. He told me how he had started his research in 1977 with a motor bike, a sheep dog, and a .308 rifle. "Dog sat on the petrol tank as I putted along, then he'd leap off the bike when he got a dose of pig up his nostrils!" I learned that feral pigs in Australia, as in many parts of the world, were the wild descendants of pigs brought to the country by European colonials. The exceptions, he said, might be the very pigs we were now hunting. "In Queensland, I've found ticks on some pigs that are found only in New Guinea and Melanesia. And a stomach nematode found only in India and eastern Asia. The implication is that travelers brought in pigs across the Torres Strait perhaps long in advance of European settlers. But that's all circumstantial. I still have a lot of work to do."

For the first few hours, I enjoyed myself. I was with a man who genuinely loved his work, and that kind of enthusiasm is conta-gious. Also, we were in big forest. I guessed some of the trees to be more than a hundred feet tall. They stood on massive plank buttresses that were a cascade of jade vines. There were clear-water streams to ford and the air was fresh. "Oh, you'll see places that few locals and no tourists have ever seen," Pavlov had promised, and he was certainly right.

But then the terrain changed, and my mood began to change with it. The grade became steeper, jagged with rock, and still we climbed, chasing the dogs. Worse, the undergrowth became dom-inated by a particularly noxious plant that Australians call "wait-awhile palm." I have never in my life experienced anything like wait-awhile palm and I hope to God I never experience it again.

The wait-awhile palm starts life as a vine that is serrated by thorns shaped like fishhooks. This vine shoots out in tendrils, tangling itself with other wait-awhile vines until the whole mess resembles concertina wire. The mountain was covered with it, but that didn't deter Pavlov or his dogs. ("Pigs are smart, mate! Exactly the kind of country where they choose to hide by day.") I would take a step and the vines would trip my leg. As I was untangling my leg, the fishhooks would latch into my hands, then tangle around my arms. For three hours, maybe four, I never took an unencumbered stride. I tried finessing my way through it, then I tried bulling my way, but one was no better than the other. It was maddening. It was exhausting. My calves began to cramp. Then my thighs. When I tried to yawn, my jaw cramped, too. And still we pushed toward the top of the mountain.

Pavlov was wearing shorts; his legs were a bloody mess. He didn't seem to mind or even notice. I began to study his expression, his demeanor, to see if he was subjecting me to some kind of trial by fire. If so, he wasn't the only one around who knew how to use an M1 carbine! Exhausted or not, I could squeeze off a get-even lethal round or two, not a problem. And if his dogs turned ugly, I'd give them something more memorable than a pig up the nostrils!

But no, Pavlov was a pure spirit. This was his work and he was obsessed by it. Ego and comfort had no more meaning to him than those bastard vines, which is to say that he was unlike any field researcher I had ever met. He was not of a type; the man's behavior was contrary to all my previous conditioning. Because you can bet your last bottom dollar on this: If I had not met a field researcher like Piggy Pavlov, I would have been sipping a beer at the eco lodge pool, or blissfully watching the Toyotas fly by on the coastal road—anywhere but on that hellish mountain.

We came to another stream and I dropped down into it, drinking deeply. I couldn't go on. I was cramping like a narcosis victim; my electrolyte meter was at dead empty. Yet I couldn't make myself admit it to Pavlov. He had told me "You must have a very high tolerance for inconvenience to hunt pigs," and I had laughed off the warning. But enough was enough! I opened my mouth to speak the truth but, instead, a lie floated out. I croaked, "I've been thinking about it, Piggy, and I'm almost sure that I got a whiff of hogs back by the truck. Pretty strong, too."

Isn't it amazing how controlled we can sound when we are least in control of our senses? But Pavlov never doubted me; never doubted me for an instant. He said, "There *was* a lot of sign down there, mate. But are you certain?"

I told him that I had spent part of my boyhood working on a hog farm—and that, at least, was true. "The smell of pigs sticks with a man," I told him. "I would have said something earlier, but I thought the dogs might be onto something fresh."

Pavlov mustered the troops, "Kazi! Heckle! Meat!" and we immediately started back down the mountain. I could have wept with relief. Maybe I did. Or maybe it was just having to fight my way back through those goddamn vines. It took almost as much time to get down as it did to hike up, but we made it. There would be no pigs waiting for us, of course, but it didn't matter. Not to me, it didn't. I had done what few others had done— hunted with Peter Pavlov—and I had done it without whining or quitting. Not officially, anyway. But, wonder of wonders, as we walked into the clearing that led to the truck, a big boar and four sows jumped out, and a very pleased Piggy shot two of them.

Later, as we performed the necropsies, Pavlov paid me a compliment. "You've got a nose for this, mate. Hog farm was it? Fair dinkum, you do!"

I told him that it was conditioning. When it came to pigs, I was like a fighter answering the bell. . . .

Darwin Town

After only a week in Australia's Northern Territory, mostly hanging around Darwin, I caught myself emulating the strange ceremony of a much-traveled friend of mine.

"Am I so odd?" he once asked me.

Friendship can tolerate anything but joint boat ownership or deceit. "You're odd," I told him kindly. "You didn't believe those doctors? Fine. But this is your *buddy* talking."

No matter where he goes in the world—particularly if it's some ratty, lonely place—here is what he does: He makes inquiries into the price of real estate even though he has no plans to relocate. He studies the local architecture and selects a good place to build. Along with constructing an imaginary house, he also computes the kind and quality of the imaginary life he would enjoy there. My friend's needs are simple. They have been calculated in rupees, pesos, pounds, and African shillings, taxes dutifully included.

My friend tried to explain himself once, suggesting that I had not yet discovered that travel consumes as surely as it compensates, implying that I didn't yet have a "profound" travel experience under my belt.

Enough Prozac under the belt was more like it. "Just thank the good Lord they don't test for dementia at border crossings," I counseled him. "There are lepers who would have more frequent-flier miles than you."

Not that my friend was with me in Darwin. No. For the last several weeks, I'd been traveling around Australia and had ended up in the Northern Territory without any guidance from him. There was Queensland, which was green and steamy and tropical, and there was Tasmania, which was cool and forested and gorgeous. I had included Darwin in the itinerary for the sanest of reasons: I had never been there before, so why not go?

The brochures flogged Darwin as a "modern port on the Timor Sea," and recommended aboriginal rock paintings, "jumping crocodiles," and the desert "Red Centre" of Alice Springs as primary attractions. I found it heartening that a region as gigantic as the Northern Territory had so few tourist destinations to pitch. Even so, on final air approach, I was unprepared for the horizon of wild space and pure sea light that rims Darwin. The land had a hot, primeval aspect. Tendrils of steam wafted upward, as if the process of chemical genesis continued here. Darwin did indeed appear modern, and for good reason—it was leveled by Cyclone Tracy in 1974 so most of the high-rise hotels and office buildings were less than twenty years old. But the contrast of a city that ended abruptly at the borders of sea and plain communicated a frontier feel, as if wagons had been circled, and

Darwin Town

I was pleased with the impression that I was flying into an Australian outpost rather than into the region's largest (population 69,000) metropolitan center.

I rented a room and did daily probes. Downtown Darwin was good for jogging. There were outdoor malls, botanical gardens, and outback outfitters. In too many cities around the world, sidewalk travelers wear expressions of introspective outrage. Not in Darwin. People had a blue-collar light, as if they were just glad to live in a world that had electricity and plumbing. On February 19, 1942, ninety-three Japanese bombers, with fighter escorts, firebombed Darwin in what, even now, seems a defining moment in the city's history and a crucible of the city's character. The citizenry dug in, fought back, and kicked butt. Along with a military museum, an aviation museum, and dozens of memorial sites, Darwin retains a stiff-upper-lipped World War II flyboy attitude. Yanks are welcome. Big-band tunes are still favorites on local radio. It's a pleasant thing to lean against the antiaircraft gun at East Point Peninsula, watching wild wallabies while listening to the Andrews Sisters sing "Drinking Rum and Coca Cola."

I liked the place; I loved the people. They had gone "troppo." They were sports. They were bush hardened. They drank stubbies and threw snags on the barbie. There was a rare racial geniality: whites, blacks, East Indians, Melville Islanders—you name it. Everyone but the enemy was accepted, and the enemy just wasn't around anymore. The only tyranny was isolation. Strangers were the antidote for that.

The guys at the tackle shop insisted I go fishing. A business leader invited me into his home and squired me around. I happened to mention to a local reporter that I was interested in baseball. Two hours later, I was out at Wanguri Park, catching infield, wearing a Northern Territory ball cap, and trading stories with the senior all-star coaches. The Darwin Yacht Club allowed me in for sunset tea even though I had never belonged to any yacht club anywhere in my life ("What the hell, ya look like a decent sort") and an aboriginal family that lived shelterless on Fannie Bay Beach invited me to eat when I stupidly jogged through their luncheon ("You like fish, we bet!"). Within just a few days it seemed that I had met just about everyone there was to meet, and that I had been welcomed, if not adopted, unconditionally.

In time, I began to probe outward, beyond the city limits and into the outback. But can you blame me? I kept returning to Darwin.

I became interested in the Mary River wetlands that lie east of the Adelaide River and east and southeast of Darwin. When locals spoke of the Mary River, they always lowered their voices just a little, as if taking me into their confidence to share a secret. The Magella Plains of Kakadu National Park were more famous, they said. Kakadu attracted nearly two hundred thousand visitors a year. But they assured me that the Mary River flood plain was equally spectacular in terms of topography and wildlife. Better yet, it was seldom visited by outsiders.

"It's because the best part of the Mary is mostly private property," I was told. "It's got more crocs, birds, and fish than Kakadu. You have to live here to know about it. And you need permission to have a look."

I learned that the man who controlled one of the largest sections of the Mary River flood plain was Neville Walker. Legend is a stanchion of frontier mentality; Walker was a popular local legend. In 1961, he and his buddy, Frazier Henry, decided to pluck themselves from the ranks of hired labor. They pooled their small savings, made a down payment on a road grader, and subcontracted a job near Alice Springs. They didn't have the cash to transport the grader, so they drove it—nearly nine hundred miles at fifteen miles per hour. They did the work at Alice Springs, but the contractor went bust and they didn't get paid. So they drove the grader nine hundred miles back to Darwin— where their second job went bust. Again, they didn't get paid. Broke, in debt, and tired of driving a road grader all over Australia, most people would have quit. But Henry and Walker weren't most people. Over the next three decades, the men would parlay that one piece of machinery into a booming mega-million-dollar conglomerate with international holdings. In the Northern Territory, Horatio Alger stories must include a full measure of outback sweat and stubbornness to pass muster, which is why Walker is a popular local legend.

The idea of phoning up cold to introduce myself to a VIP mogul like Walker was about as reasonable as trying to direct dial the CEO of U.S. Steel, but that's what I did. I expected Walker to be standoffish and suspicious. Instead, he clapped me on the back and toured me around in his Toyota four-by-four. Yes, he had holdings that included the Mary River wetlands. He controlled about 1,500 square kilometers, from the Timor Sea deep into the outback.

Nine hundred square miles?

Yep. "You won't believe the amount of wildlife out there," Walker told me. "The birds, the wallabies, the crocs—it's truly extraordinary. A magnificent place. Thing is, I'm a bit worried about it. We've been having a spot of trouble out there."

Walker sat me down and, with a map and photographs, familiarized me with the dynamics. The Mary River wasn't a river as such. It was the drainage conduit for a vast grassy flood plain. During the monsoon wet season (October to April), the river and its feeder creeks drained tens of thousands of hectares snaking along to the sea. During the dry season, the river separated into a series of still-water ponds, or billabongs, providing a water source for wildlife. But now the Timor Sea had begun to intrude farther and farther into these billabongs, dispersing fauna and had already killed 17,000 hectares of wetland flora. The major cause of the saltwater intrusion, Walker told me, was the Asian water buffalo. The water buffalo was introduced to Australia in 1826 and had flourished in the wild. (There were once tens of thousands of feral buffalo roaming the Mary River flood plain, but most of them were shot—or rounded up and inoculated—during the recent Brucellosis and Tuberculosis Eradication Campaign.) But during their century-and-a-half reign, the water buffalo had trampled out deep gutters between the sea and the grasslands. Those gutters had finally become a watercourse into the interior, which is why salt water was now intruding into the system.

In an effort to reclaim the region, private landowners such as Walker, along with the Northern Territory Conservation Commission, were in the process of constructing earthen dikes, or barrages, to stay the flow of salt water. They were also battling another exotic intruder, the South American mimosa bush that, like the water buffalo, was impacting the entire wetland system.

"The potential of the Northern Territory is immense," Walker told me. "The only reason it's not yet tapped is that we lack population—only a hundred and seventy thousand people in an area that takes up a sixth of all Australia. But Indonesia and all of Asia are beginning to awaken, and Darwin is closer to Jakarta than it is to Sydney. One day we'll be the southern gateway to Asia, and you can wager we won't suffer a lack of population then. When that day comes, I think it would be very wise to have our environmental problems under control so that treasures like the Mary River can thrive, not just survive."

The next day, I drove a dusty hundred kilometers (the last twenty of it on a one-lane sand road) to the Mary River dock where Nobby Muhsam fixed me up with a pontoon boat, a chart, and sent me on my way. I found it odd that the deck of the boat was enclosed with welded grating—until I got out onto the river and saw the number of estuarine crocodiles. Crocodiles were everywhere, basking on the bank, hanging motionless in the dark water. I have been on rivers far prettier than the Mary. It appeared to be little more than a drainage ditch choked with giant lily pads. But never in my life have I been in stranger, more seductive terrain. On all sides, a vast grass veld spread away to the horizon. When clouds shifted, the color of the veld changed in slow synch: from brown to copper to gold. This was in the spring, the end of the dry season, and a hot kiln wind blew down out of the sun. It was a leaching wind, deadly dry, but the river was a water stronghold and a magnate to every living thing for miles. There were wading birds and hawks and anhingas and parrots by the thousands. Magpie geese flushed in a haze of black and white. As I puttered along, I got a glimpse of a water buffalo in the distance . . . and maybe a wallaby, too. I couldn't be sure.

When the river deadened, I wanted to climb out of the boat and keep going. But there were the crocs, all those crocs. Yet I wanted to see more. The flood plains of the Mary River were what I imagined the Earth to be at the beginning of time. Only sixty miles from Darwin, I had arrived at the very back of beyond.

Neville Walker's sons, David and Clint, and their pilot buddy, Mark Grosvenor, lived in a stilt-house bachelor quarters on a cattle station in the middle of nowhere. They wore Akubras, rode horses, mustered cattle, and carried revolvers. They also flew helicopters, did their own cooking, and communicated with civilization via single-side band radio. All in their early twenties, they were big, fit, and happy with their roustabout cowboy lives. The only thing the outback didn't provide them was alluded to by a sign on the living room wall: *Girls Wanted For Various Positions*.

"Meant to take that silly thing down," David Walker said when he noticed me staring. "Bit embarrassing when we get company." But then he grinned. "Thing is, we don't get much company!"

I had traveled to this remote station—Woolner Station by name—because it was close to the sea, though a part of the Mary River flood plain, and my day on the river had primed me to see more. I wanted to get an overview of the region. I wanted to see all those birds and crocodiles from the air and also while standing knee-deep in grass. That's what travelers are supposed to do, right? Zero in on the bounty of a place and drink it all in?

Exactly. It is our compensation for all the crummy connections and our ghostly wanderings—and "ghostly" sums up the normal condition of a traveler, does it not? We drop down into foreign places but are never a part of that place, and we interact with foreign people yet separate ourselves with a gauze of awareness and constant observation. We are visual bounty hunters, on the track of that which is different. But in the end it is only we who are different; different because we don't belong and will soon be leaving.

In the Northern Territory, around Darwin, particularly on the flood plains of the Mary River, it wasn't that way. Not for me it wasn't. When I raved to Neville Walker about what I had experienced on my boat trip, he said something interesting. Said it a little shyly: "Truth is, Randy, I've been trying to figure a way that we could let other people see what you've seen. In a limited way—I don't want any resorts out there. There's too much nesting ground. The place is just too delicate. But if we could come up with a way that a few folks could do a spot of bird watching, maybe a little fishing . . ."

I took the remark as inclusionary. The problem became personal. Which is probably why I had so much fun roaming around and flying over the region with David, Mark, and Clint. Once, hovering in the Bell 47 helicopter at seven hundred feet, Mark said to me, "You think Americans would be keen on this?"

I could look one direction and see a herd of water buffalo. Below us, there was the papier-mâché bloom of geese and storks. Ahead, there was Van Diemen Gulf and about a trillion wading birds. Keen? There were Audubon people who would fight bare fisted to see this place.

Another time, we banked down low over a billabong to count crocodiles, and I yelled to Mark, "There are tarpon in that pond!"

He shrugged. "There're tarpon in all the billabongs, mate. Loads. But wouldn't fishermen worry about being eaten? The crocs, I mean."

Sensible fishermen, perhaps. But not fly fishermen. Fly fishermen would be willing to risk it—particularly after hearing about the barramundi and bonefish I'd seen rooting off the beach.

That's how it went: looking, planing, trying to figure out a way to open the region a little without using it up. The Northern Territory was still young. It was the new frontier—Neville Walker had said as much. Here, perhaps, there was time and concern and knowledge enough to do things right.

I felt a part of that. I did, I really did—for a short time, anyway. Although maybe my old friend was correct when he said that travel consumes as surely as it compensates because, one Darwin dusk, drinking a sunset beer at Stokes Hill Wharf, it felt perfectly natural for me to look out past the harbor lights and to ask, "Is it tough to immigrate here?" And to later say, "I found this great place to build . . . "

The Sharks of Lake Nicaragua

For many years, Nicaragua has taken pride in having what was in past years claimed to be the only land-locked population of freshwater sharks in the world. They were said to have been trapped when a bay of the Pacific Ocean was cut off by volcanic action and filled by rain. . . .

—Thomas B. Thorson, *The Impact of Commercial Exploitation on Sawfish and Shark Populations in Lake Nicaragua*, 1982, American Fisheries Society

I first sensed the potential for trouble in Nicaragua about a year after the war, when I chased a pig up the steps of a cathedral toward the open doors of what might have been the sacred vestry. The pig was smart; a vestry was exactly the safe harbor he would have chosen. But participants in the wedding that had just ended were not amused, and who can blame them?

There they stood, men in guayabera shirts, women in their finery, bride and groom, maids and ushers, spilling out over the banks of steps that led up to the stone basilica. Maybe they were throwing rice, maybe the bride was about to toss the bouquet. I can't say—I was watching the pig. Then here we came, zigzagging through the wedding party, a squealing swine with a 215-pound gringo in hot pursuit, one perhaps headed for the sanctuary of the chapel, the other realizing, too late, headed for trouble.

This was in Grenada, Nicaragua's most beautiful city, where herding cloven-hoofed animals through cathedrals is generally discouraged. Grenada is an ancient municipality of cobbled streets, open markets, marble columns, and ornate parks, everything filmed by a layer of grime and the shadow of this Central American nation's withering poverty. But there is a nice Castilian light to the town; a cosmopolitan savvy not found anywhere else in the country. Grenada is located an hour southeast of Managua on the shore of Lake Nicaragua, the twentieth largest lake in the world. I hadn't come to Grenada to chase pigs, of course—who would plan such a thing? I came because of a long interest in the freshwater sharks of Lake Nicaragua. For years, these sharks were thought to be a unique species (known for a time as *Carcharhinus nicaraguensis*); a sweet water anomaly caused by the same volcanic cataclysm, it was thought, that had severed this ancient water bed from the sea. It wasn't until the 1970s, through the work of American Dr. Thomas B. Thorson, that it was demonstrated that at least some of the sharks migrated from the Caribbean, traveling 120 miles of jungle river and rapids to get to the lake. I had never been able to find much information about them but, in recent years, I had heard nothing at all, and it was my plan to talk with fishermen, to visit the wholesale markets, to fish for the shark myself, and see firsthand how the animal was faring.

Grenada, which is the lake's main port, was our first stop. Well, actually our second. We had landed at Augusto Sandino International Airport in Managua a couple of days earlier, flying in over the Caribbean coast where we expected to see jungle. Instead, beneath the flight corridor, were the broad squares of planted fields, inlaid like green tiles between dirt roads and rivers. Managua, a city of more than one million people, appeared as a fringe of slum housing—rough shacks thrown together in random jumbles so dense that they did not disappear from view until the plane touched down.

At the airport, we rented a Toyota Land Cruiser, a beige four-wheel drive with air-conditioning we did not use. We probably should have used the air-conditioning while making our way through Managua, for Third World cities—the sounds and smells and sights—are interchangeable, and not pleasant. Poverty has an odor, and so does desperation, and one does not want to be reminded of those things while riding in a $23,000 vehicle.

But rural Central America is different. Rural Central America smells unlike anyplace I have ever been, and I wanted the windows down. For nearly all that there is to see can be found in the air as well: wood smoke from cooking fires, cattle pastures and fruit stands, diesel fumes of public buses, the saturated earth smells of jungle rivers. Here, the land still makes itself known.

After a couple days in Managua spent going to baseball games (Nicaraguans have two great passions, I had heard—baseball and poetry) we made the drive to Grenada, which is where I had that unfortunate experience with the hog. I was walking the sidewalk, comforted and gratified by the many friendly greetings I was receiving—me, an undisguisable American—when I noticed a distraught boy chasing a pig through the busy street. This was no playful romp. The boy was upset. The pig was determined. So I joined right in.

We crazy-legged our way through traffic, the pig and I, with the boy right behind—I could hear his yells of encouragement ("¡Ándale, gringo, ándale!"). A boulevard slowed the pig a little. I gained ground. Then a donkey cart nearly hit me, and the pig gained that ground right back again. It's fun chasing animals, of course, but dangerous, too, because a loose pig requires one's full attention. I did not hear the whoops of scattering maids and ushers, nor sense their disapproval, and it wasn't until the pig made a clattering turn toward the doors of the church that I realized I was now on grounds not sanctified for these high jinx. Also, I had drawn a crowd.

The pig bolted for the altar inside, and I made a desperate lunge to head him off, thinking, *Oh Lord, make that pig have a heart attack,* but He didn't. Yet the pig didn't go inside, either. It headed back out into traffic where a bus missed him, but the boy didn't.

My first night in Grenada, I went looking for the boy. Had I found him, I would have given him a baseball.

Along with gear for catching sharks, baseballs were among the things I took to Nicaragua. A dozen baseballs, five uniform jerseys, and two gloves, were stashed in among the fishing reels and wire leader. Just prior to my leaving, my two sons made a surprising announcement: They had decided not to play Little League this year. The season was just too long. They were right, and I supported their decision, but I was disappointed, too. I like baseball. I still play it. Baseball, not softball; the game where catchers strap on the gear and hitters need helmets. That my sons had already tired of the game was oddly disturbing, though I believe I succeeded in not showing it. With their consent, I collected the uniforms they had outgrown, the oldest of their many gloves, then went to the garage and, from the buckets of balls, chose twelve good ones. I considered taking a few bats, or maybe a set of catcher's gear. Though Nicaragua had, at the time, only one player in the Major Leagues (Expos pitcher Dennis Martinez), I knew that baseball is Nicaragua's national game, and these things might be nice gifts for the children I met. But I also had to travel light, and the shark gear took precedence, so I took only the balls, the gloves, and the uniforms.

In Grenada, the China Nica restaurant became our unofficial headquarters. It has a pleasant open courtyard and, for reasons I never determined, played a half dozen American surfing-era songs over and over again (I had yet to see another American in the country, so it wasn't to draw the tourist trade). The restaurant's main attraction was a huge set of shark jaws on the wall—taken from a shark caught in the lake, we were told. It is now generally accepted that the freshwater sharks of Nicaragua are bull sharks, *Carcharhinus leucas*, known by a variety of names worldwide. It is a tough, aggressive animal, implicated in attacks on bathers and skin divers. In Africa, where it is known as the Zambezi River shark, it feeds so vigorously and indiscriminately that some municipalities have laid nets to protect their beaches.

I had heard anecdotal accounts of attacks in the lake, though well aware that ferocity ascribed to sharks is more accurately a projection of human qualities the animals neither have nor need. Even so, these jaws were impressive: a mouth opening nearly thirty inches high and nineteen inches wide. Bull sharks are thought not to exceed ten feet in length and four hundred pounds. I have caught and released specimens nearly that large, and their mouth framework was markedly smaller than the trophy hanging on the wall—but if it was really taken from a Nicaraguan bull shark, I had no way of knowing.

We met interesting people at the China Nica restaurant, but always received conflicting accounts when we asked about the sharks. A few people told us that yes, there were sharks in the lake, still plenty of sharks. But most told us that the sharks were gone—a disappointing thing to hear for someone who had come so far to see them. I would have discounted the reports, but we found no sharks in the fish markets, and the sellers there explained that most of the sharks around Grenada had been taken for their meat and fins in the 1970s (Japanese buyers began to solicit worldwide in the mid-seventies, carrying to remote sea places pamphlets that showed exactly how to take and preserve the fins). We were told two processing plants had thrived during that decade and finally folded in 1981, but not before marketing more than four million pounds of meat and fins. Even so, I was told, there might still be a few sharks at the southern base of the lake, into which the San Juan River fed.

Dr. Norman López, whom we met at the restaurant, agreed that the village of San Carlos on the southeastern shore of the lake, or the Solentiname Islands—a cluster of more than thirty isolated islands west of San Carlos—might be the best place to access the fish. "Those places are not so busy as Grenada," López told me, "though there are more people now that the war refugees are coming back from Costa Rica." López is a physician not a fisherman, but he is intimately familiar with the outback regions of Nicaragua—and the status of refugees—because he works with indigenous peoples such as the Sumus, Ramas, and Miskitos. These people were described as "the wild men of the swamps" by Conquistador Don Francisco Hernández who, in 1523, claimed the region, because they created a shield of native resistance the Spanish never conquered. But it was this same fierce independence that brought them under the guns of the Sandinistas during the recent war—an outright attempt at genocide, according to some. Not that Dr. López told me this, no. "I am a physician, not a politician," he said. Yet it is impossible to avoid politics while in Nicaragua, for its history has been a tragedy of intrigue, outside manipulation, and revolt since it declared its independence in 1838 then immediately suffered its first civil war—a war between the wealthy conservative families of Grenada and wealthy liberal families of León. These two factions, though sharded and branched dozens of times, provided the prop roots of a war that would crackle along for one hundred fifty years; a war that always called upon the peasantry to do the actual fighting and dying; a war that, in time, would provide a playing field for the world's major economic powers.

Nicaragua is now a shaky democracy, but politics still permeates all aspects of Nicaraguan life. Even its baseball. While in Managua, I had watched the country's most popular team, the Boer, and the country's least popular team, the Dantos. The Boer drew thousands of fans; the Dantos a few dozen. I was told the Boer team was popular because it was the traditional adversary of the Somoza family team (a team which disbanded because its players were killed or imprisoned by the Sandinistas). Yet the Dantos *is* the Sandinista team. Even though the Sandinistas still control the country's army and its media, baseball fans, at least, seem to make a point of snubbing their team—a paradox that nicely illustrates the paradox of Nicaraguan politics.

> The presence of sharks and sawfish in Lake Nicaragua and its drainage system, the Río San Juan, has been known to the outside world since early in the time of the Spanish conquest. . . .
>   There have been long-standing differences as to whether [they] are actually marine sharks that make their way through the river or are landlocked by a series of rapids and therefore represent a distinct, iso-lated species or subspecies.
> —Thomas B. Thorson with Donald E. Watson and
> C. Michael Cowan, *The Status of the Freshwater*
> *Shark of Lake Nicaragua*, Copeia, 1966

The car trip from Grenada to San Carlos, a journey of about two hundred miles, isn't for the faint of heart. And not just because the roads are bad, though they are. The road map the rental car lady gave us was nearly useless—the whole thing reduced to the point that it was unreadable. The road map I had brought from the states was better—but not much. I thought the map showed a road that skirted Lake Nicaragua. But no such road exists. (It was the mapmaker's way of highlighting the lake, though why nearly five thousand square miles of water requires definition, I don't know.) We made our first wrong turn at Tapitapa. Or maybe it was Tisma—I'm still not sure.

We made our way north on the PanAmerican Highway, then turned on the road to San Jacinto. I do not know what road it was. The roads are not marked. But it was there, and I took it. It was a good road, too, in hindsight, though I did not think it at the time. The potholes were readily visible, and there were children along the way to smile at. The countryside was beaten brown by the wind and the mountains were bare—similar to the American West, one of us remarked.

Below Acoyapa, though, we were educated in the way of Nicaraguan roads. The road was wide, but only because of decades that drivers had spent trying to skirt this hellish bed of wild rock and crevices. There was little commerce here, so the few houses were built of bamboo or scrap planking, the roofs of palm thatch sloped like pyramids. In the yards, naked children tottered among goats and dozing horses. And every few miles or so, I noted the worn footpaths of makeshift baseball diamonds. One such field was in a trash dump—one of the few flat places available—where more than two dozen boys played using bare hands and an old ball mended with black electrical tape. I stopped and watched their game for a few minutes before lobbing a new white ball to the pitcher. This was an unprecedented event—I could read it in their faces; a look of wonderment and pure joy that I carried with me down that bastard road.

I am certainly not recommending it, but it is my practice, while traveling, to pick up hitchhikers. I consider it a courtesy to the country that is my unwitting host, and it's nice to see new faces on the intimate terms my bad Spanish seems to require. I picked up two lady hitchhikers outside Juigalpa. They carried bags of rice and onions—they had been to market. The ladies giggled a lot. A few miles below Acoyapa, I stopped to pick up a lone man. I stopped as much to pick him up, I think, as I did to give my ears and body a rest from the noise and jarring. But when I stopped, three ladies and a small boy who were sitting in the shade piled in as well. It was crowded in our vehicle, I can tell you, people sitting shoulder to elbow, the produce of three families stacked upon our personal gear, and the people stacked upon that. How far were they going? They could not make me understand, so I just drove. I drove and drove, both hands on the jolting steering wheel, the Toyota bucking beneath us. I tried different speeds. Slow was bad. Slow loosed the joints and made one's jaw ache from the anticipation of the next crater ahead. I tried fast, which was better, but only because the gullies were upon us before our nervous systems had time to react. It gave the mind a little peace, though the body suffered just as much.

We encountered three roadblocks, where soldiers were checking papers.

"Looking for revolutionaries," one man told us, though if that is true I cannot say. Only twice did the soldiers stop us. The first time, the soldiers were friendly. They smiled a lot. They wished us good day. The second time, near San Miguelito, the soldiers did not smile. There were two young boys sitting on boxes behind the soldiers, and they did not smile, either. When I caught their eye, they looked away, embarrassed. One soldier, with his automatic rifle slung barrel toward the ground, studied our papers for a long time. Many minutes, it seemed, and I did not like the look in his eye. I had the impression he wished there was some reason he could detain us.

Or perhaps I was just paranoid with fatigue from that road. It is a distressing thing to be exhausted by a road after only twenty miles, knowing you still have sixty more to go. Certainly, the road would get better?

It didn't. Though it was the dry season, a light rain fell intermittently and, over one hill, we came to a section of what looked to be gray mud. I was not going fast—hell, it was impossible to go fast on such a thing—and I'm very glad that I was not. The mud was marl clay, slick as ice. The Toyota fishtailed slightly and began to slide sideways. Had I been going fast, we certainly would have rolled—an ugly thing to consider in a vehicle as crowded and as lively as ours.

"Hey," one of us said, "that guy just upchucked back there."

"On the road?"

"No, in the car. One of our hitchhikers. Just now, he vomited."

By then I could smell it. Where were the soldiers and their guns when we needed them?

The worst part, though, was crossing the bridges. Around a narrow bend, we came to a gorge created by the Tepenaguasapi River, a natural barrier if there ever was one. Rough planks, spaced the precise width of our tires, created a single lane across the river. There was no guard rail to interrupt the view of the green water fifty feet below. Not that I looked; no way. The only thing I saw was my knuckles white on the steering wheel, and those planks. The bridge over the Río Camastro was nearly as bad and, by the time we got to the Río Tule, it didn't much matter. I was numb. Numb from the road and the balancing act those bridges required.

The drive from Grenada to San Carlos took us seven hours. The only stops we made were for hitchhikers, and once when I passed a boy wearing an ancient baseball glove. In the rearview mirror I could see him waving, so I stopped and gave him a baseball. Indeed, there was no other reason to stop, for there were no stores or rest places of any kind. Once we slowed for a procession of people carrying a plastic litter down the hillside. A pair of brown feet protruded from the plastic, rigid as wood.

"Muerto," said one of the passengers, the man who had been sick.

Dead. Yes, undoubtedly. A half dozen men and women, their faces expressionless, clothes ragged, carrying a corpse wrapped in bright blue plastic—coming from jungle only to disappear into jungle, as numb to their task as I now was to mine.

Strangely, the funeral procession rallied our sick hitchhiker's spirits, and he left us at some unmarked crossroads with a cheerful "Adiós," never mentioning the mess he had made.

Finally, just after sunset, through a gloom of dusk and the smoke of cooking fires, we raised the lights of San Carlos, a lake village of a few thousand souls.

> Since the time that the rapids were purported to block the path of the sharks, an English fleet of 50 ships . . . ascended the river as far as El Castillo in 1762. . . . Furthermore, in 1849, Commodore Vanderbilt established an interocean transit line [up the river to the lake]

across Nicaragua to transport prospectors to the
California gold fields.

—Thorson, *Explorers Journal*, 1978

Day or night, San Carlos is a spirited, lively place, and perhaps it
has always been so. In the 1800s, it was through San Carlos that
gold-hungry Americans traveled, on their way to the California
gold rush, transported over water and land by Cornelius
Vanderbilt's Accessory Transit Company. Vanderbilt made more
than one million dollars in his company's first year—then refused
to pay the small duty due Nicaragua. It was through San Carlos
that Britain and the United States tried to negotiate the building
and joint ownership of a canal that would link the Caribbean
and Pacific (when negotiations stalled, the U.S. secretly hammered out a deal with Panama). It was near San Carlos that
adventurer, despot William Walker operated and sowed the seeds
of his undoing. Walker, a Napoleon-sized redhead, was a failed
journalist, abolitionist, and raving liberal who, in 1850, formed
his own army and attacked northern Mexico in an effort to
democratize it but, instead, only helped buffalo it into selling
what is now southern Arizona to the United States. Outraged,
Walker sailed to Nicaragua, where he mustered another army and
joined the pro-democratic liberals of León in their war against
the conservatives of Grenada. Walker and his small army (The
Immortals) fought so ferociously and successfully that he was
appointed head of the Nicaraguan army. Walker immediately did
what several generals have done since—named himself President
of Nicaragua. He declared English the official language and ruled
with a bully's enthusiasm until he seized Vanderbilt's Accessory

Transit Company—a fatal error, for it invited U.S. intervention. Walker was executed by firing squad, and it wasn't until 1909 that the apparently endless wars and intrigue between Nicaraguan liberals and conservatives once again brought U.S. intervention in the form of three thousand marines. The U.S. maintained a military force in the country until 1933 when, pressured by public opinion and guerrilla hero Augusto Sandino, troops were withdrawn, leaving a U.S. puppet government ruled by a man who called himself "The Last Marine": Anastasio (Tacho) Somoza. About Somoza, Franklin Roosevelt said, "He may be a sonofabitch, but he's our sonofabitch." The same could be said of Somoza's two sons, who came to power after their father's death.

It was Somoza, aided by his close ties to Roosevelt and inspired by his love of U.S. culture, who helped bring baseball to Nicaragua. As a backhanded reminder of Tacho's contribution, the national baseball stadium in Managua is named for the deranged clergyman who assassinated him: Mad Monk Stadium.

San Carlos is a fun place, but it is still hard to associate this dead-end town with so much history. The main street, which skirts the waterfront, is always noisy with people and music, horses, pigs, sellers, buyers, and small boys throwing firecrackers. I have never been to a place where firecrackers are so popular. I watched one small boy, no older than eight, using the cigarette he was smoking to light firecrackers, which he then threw at passing horses. Adults smiled and rebuked him in a gentle way.

On the lakefront, where city sewage bubbles out in viscous globs, pangas and dugout canoes were forever loading and unloading while women washed clothes on rocks bleached white from generations of use. In the merchant stalls, vendors offered many things for sale: melons, bananas, onions, fish, pig snouts, beef joints, Japanese radios, and small televisions. But no sharks—again we were given conflicting stories. That sharks had been decimated in the 1970s; the sharks were still there, and we would certainly find them around the lake's islands.

The main market was an open building of wood and tin, dark as a cave inside, where there were more small stalls, more pro-duce from the countryside. Outside this busy place a man hailed us in cheerful English: "How you doin', guys?" He was a young black man, dressed in a black Marlboro T-shirt, and when I'd asked where he'd learned the language, he said, "Me? I'm English, too!" By which he meant that he was from Bluefields, Nicaragua's main Caribbean port, where, because it was once under British colonial rule, the peasantry—Miskitos and Sumas, mostly—still speak English.

The man's name was George Brooks, and he sat with a smaller man who wore pink polish on his nails and who, according to Brooks, worked for the local Sandinista radio station—which seemed a curious alliance when George told us how he happened to be in San Carlos.

"I come here to make some bucks," he said, "but there're no bucks here, man. Figured since the war was over, there might be work, but no way. I been spending the last few years in the jun-gle, running from the soldiers. They wanted me to fight for them, man, but not me."

Which side? I wanted to know.

His grin told me how naive I was. "Both sides, man. They both chase me, want me to fight. My brother, they shot him and killed him because he wouldn't fight. My father, too. Me, I went to the jungle, running. They blew up our boat, but all I got was this burn on my face and a bullet scar on my head."

The burn scar was plain to see, a coagulated mass of skin the size of an orange on his left cheek, though he had to part his hair to show us the bullet wound. "The Sandinistas did that, man. They didn't like me. Hell, they don't even like each other. Only ones worse than them was the Cubans. Maybe the Russians, only I didn't meet no Russians."

So he sympathized with the Contras?

"Me, I'm not for either one of them. Contras bad, too. That's why I been hiding in the jungle for the last ten years."

Wasn't it a curious thing, then, for him to be keeping company with a Sandinista radio announcer?

"Ah, that shit's over for most the people," Brooks explained. "Now we all just looking for work. Trying to make some bucks. Don't you think this'd be a good place for a couple big sports-fishing boats? Tourist center, that kind of thing? I could run something like that if I just had the bucks." It was less a statement than an inquiry. Maybe we could finance the project?

Brooks kept us company while we waited for the launch that left twice daily to the Solentiname Islands—a panga of about thirty-two feet built of mismatched boards and a tin roof with a hand-crank inboard diesel engine. He kept us entertained with grim stories of the sharks that come up the Río San Juan and eat small children. "In the villages, whenever a child is missing, they go hunt the sharks. Once I see them bring up a big shark long as this building. They cut the thing open—it stink, man—and inside we find an arm with a ring on it, and we find that little girl. She green, man, from being in there."

It was a story lent credence by a paper on the sharks published by Dr. Thorson in 1978. "In 1852," Dr. Thorson wrote, "the first United States minister to Nicaragua said that '. . . sharks abound in the lake.' They are called 'tigrones' from their rapacity. Instances are known of their having attacked and killed bathers within a stone's throw of the beach at Grenada."

It was Brooks who also told us that robbers had been stopping cars on the bad road back to Managua. "They wait by the bridges, man, when the cars have to slow. Last week they stop five cars and buses."

This was not good news to me, for I was already worried about the Toyota we had rented. I had stupidly refused to pay for the Budget rental insurance out of long habit from refusing it in safer places around the world, and now I couldn't get the car started. If I couldn't get it back to Managua, would they make me pay for the thing before allowing me to return to the States? Bandits, armed thugs, child-eating sharks, an uninsured $23,000 vehicle all could have worked in concert to make me hate the place— and I might have hated it if the people we met weren't so unfailingly kind (we later learned that Brooks was exaggerating an isolated robbery) yet, stuffed into the narrow lunch, my big legs folded over bags of rice, I wondered dourly why in the hell I was forever attracted to such places.

On the boat, I met a man from Britain, Al Oliver. Oliver, thirty-two, was in Nicaragua sponsored, in part, by the British trade union for which he worked. He told me he was there to establish links between British and Nicaraguan unions, and also to participate in what he called "solidarity work." Oliver had also been in Nicaragua during the war, he said, attracted by something in the Nicaraguan revolution that had caught his imagination. "I was attracted to the underdog Sandinistas try-ing to withstand the bullying of a giant in the form of the U.S.," he said.

The giants who had armed the Sandinistas weren't bullies?

Well, that had to do with the fight against imperialism. Was I in Nicaragua because I had politics?

When I traveled I had no politics, I told him. There were other things to talk about: birds and Nicaraguan history, the smell of the boat and what we would do if this dangerously over-crowded craft, which had no life jackets or fire extinguisher, began to founder. The panga trip to the remote Solentiname takes three hours, and I didn't want to spend it talking politics. Besides, I liked Al with his dry British humor, his bright red hair plaited into braid, and his T-shirt that read: "The Revolution Continues!"

"You know who you look like?" I suggested to him. "William Walker."

I was glad Oliver took it for the joke it was, and watched his face assume a prim, humorous expression. He said, "I'm much taller than Mr. Walker," though Oliver couldn't be more than five-eight.

Myers (1952) reported a shark taken in October 1943
at Iquitos, Peru, 4000 km from the Atlantic Ocean.
—Thorson, *The Status of the Bull Shark*, Carcharhinus
leucas, *in the Amazon River*, Copeia, 1972

The Sharks of Lake Nicaragua

In 1937, the distance from the point of [the shark's capture] at Alton [Ill.] to the Gulf of Mexico was approximately 2800 km.

—Jamie E. Thomerson, Thorson, Ronald L. Hempel, *The Bull Shark*, Carcharhinus leucas, *from the Upper Mississippi River near Alton, Illinois*, Copeia, 1977

For a time, as we chugged along in the panga, a dugout canoe flying a square black sail stayed with us, running before the wind. Looking back, I could see how small San Carlos is: ledges of rusted tin and a red water tower interrupting the great encircling darkness of Lake Nicaragua. Before us, the Solentiname Islands appeared as a small dark flotilla: tree islands the size of ships.

Inside our boat, a hammock made of feed sacks was slung over the engine. Once the pilot got us under way, he stretched out in the thing, leaving the steering to one of his underlings. The quarters were close and, though the wind was fresh, it could not dilute the stronger odors of body oil, diesel fumes, and cigarettes. Sitting near me was a woman holding a baby's blanket. The bodice of her worn blouse was wet: Her milk was leaking. Where is her child? I wondered. There were no infants aboard. She spoke to no one during the entire three hours of the trip, and stepped wordlessly off onto the small island that was our first stop.

Sitting before me, though, was a pretty girl in a yellow dress and her eyes, unlike the eyes of the woman with the blanket, were wildly alive. They were bright brown, filled with life. It was as if she had spent her ten or fewer years on Earth storing light. With my bulk and blue eyes, I was a curiosity to her and she wanted to flirt. As she ate rice and boiled bananas with her fingers, I took a dime from my pocket, holding it in my thumb and forefinger so that she stared into the face of Franklin Roosevelt. I passed the coin to my right hand, then opened it. Her bright eyes widened—the coin had disappeared! Was it in my left fist? No, not there, either. I touched behind her ear and produced the dime, which I gave to her. Her expression was worth far more than that thin coin.

As our boat pulled up to San Fernando Island, shy boys peered out. There is a small hotel on this island, though neither of us could figure out where it was. Certainly it was not that open hut with the thatched roof. On the chance that it was, we decided to press on to Mancarron Island, where, Al told me, exists an artist colony. Having met many shy children, and having met many artists, I prefer the company of children, but I agreed to travel onward, anyway. But first I called one of the boys down to the dock and handed him a baseball. He held it, marveling at the thing, then ran to his hut without a thank you. Within seconds, as we were pulling away, the boy was back out with two aged gloves, and I watched the children playing catch until our slow boat rounded the point of the island and they were gone.

From the water, the islands of Solentiname are as pretty as any islands I have seen in Central America. The great trees and bromeliads and cascade of vines create a fortress of green. Around the rare bend, in the brief clearings, were always one or more small huts, a panga or two, and a dugout to be left rolling in our wake. Here the world was green and golden brown beneath hazy blue sky; a haze that seemed to originate from volcanoes in the far distance. The volcanoes, the old boats, the palm-thatched huts created a feel of the primeval not lessened by the ancient cormorants and anhingas that stood with their wings outstretched, like black plaster gargoyles, staring with reptilian eyes.

On one small island, all rainforest and dense growth, howler monkeys swung out to watch us. From the boat, a man laughed and hooted at them; the howlers hooted back, a strange vocal intersecting, tribal and confrontational and somehow edged by fear—on their part, not on the man's. On the boat, we laughed at the creatures, up there hanging from the trees. From the shadows of the forest they whoofed and chattered back.

Isla Mancarron is the largest and most populated of the lake's more than thirty islands and, as Al said, it is well known for its artists and poets (it is said that Nicaragua has more poets per capita than any country in the Americas), and I feared a thriving community of self-obsessed snobs, but couldn't have been more wrong. Founded in 1967 by priest Ernesto Cardenal, the original island commune fell under an attack by the National Guard, which destroyed it as a reprisal for a 1977 raid on San Carlos. The island now has a small primitivist art gallery, a village, and a clean, simple, cheap inn. It is a pretty place. The buildings are all white-washed, the windows are screened, and the roofs are tiled. For power, the island has a generator that goes on at dusk and off at nine though, of course, there is no hot water. We found no hot water outside Managua. A pasture with a few cows and scrawny horses separates the inn from the small village on the hill, but it is only a five-minute walk.

There is no mistaking that Mancarron is a Sandinista island. As the boat dropped us at the dock, Sandinista mottoes, painted in red and black, were everywhere. Yet it was difficult to associate the war slogans with the mild, sweet people who greeted us.

Señora Blanca, with two of her four children tagging behind, showed us to our rooms. She brought us Victoria beer and food— she is an excellent country cook—while Freddie, who also works at the inn, showed us where to store our gear. Another man, Bosco, who was apparently part of the staff, joined us as we roamed the island and told us about the local fish—guapote, machaca, and mojarra. But no sharks, he said—and smiled at my obvious disappointment. Maybe around Grenada, he said. But here, they had already been fished out.

That first evening, I met Blanca's two youngest sons, Juan and Ramón. They were good-looking boys, healthy and shy, about the ages of my own two sons. Ramón was the charmer, Juan was reserved, but they both followed me to my room and watched wide-eyed as I opened my bag.

Did they like baseball? I asked them. Oh yes, they loved baseball, and they knew of Dennis Martinez, too.

Did they have a baseball? Nope. As I already knew, kids in Nicaragua used rocks wrapped in fishing line or thread in lieu of an actual ball.

I reached into my bag and handed each of them a baseball . . . then two Red Sox jerseys from last year's Little League season. Through their expressions, their pure wonderment, I shared a long-gone delight. Could such a thing really be happening? Yes, and there was more—I gave each a glove, good gloves that my sons had outgrown.

The boys disappeared on the run, into the night, leaving me to the tractor noise of the village generator and late-night reading by headlamp.

The next morning, I was awakened by thin voices: ¿Béisbol? ¿Señor? ¿Béisbol?"

At my screen stood three new boys, peering in. Beyond I could see Ramón and Juan cutting firewood in the pasture. Their new gloves were tied to their waists, they both wore Red Sox jerseys.

> The most compelling evidence on the question of Atlantic vs. Pacific origin is the simple fact that Lake Nicaragua is drained by a large, broad river, which flows into the Caribbean Sea.
>
> —Thorson, *The Status of the Freshwater Shark of Lake Nicaragua*

"That's the problem with that kind of thing," Al told me. We were eating lunch on the wooden veranda. In the great poinsettia tree that shaded us, a mynah bird made a strange warbling sound, as if blowing over a gourd flute. Al said, "You give something to one of them, they all have to have it. You can go on playing that game forever."

He was right, of course, which is why I had to refuse the three boys. The others who came later, too. I had brought only a dozen baseballs, and now there were just a few left. But certainly there was something else I could do for them.

In the afternoon I walked up to the village: neat block houses with corrugated roofs, all open so that the chickens could roam through the houses and the yards. There was a shed used as a health clinic, and we asked a man there how many children were in the village. Maybe twelve boys in all, he said.

And girls?

The girls didn't play baseball.

Down the path, a girl was watching us, and I took a ball from my belt pack and offered it to her. That quick, the boys fell in behind, for they had been watching us, too. At first she reached to take it, but then hesitated as the boys began to chide her. Then the thing was gone from my hand, and the girl watched as one of the boys darted off with it. I shrugged, she shrugged back as if it didn't matter, but I could see that it did.

All morning I had watched Juan and Ramón in their proud Red Sox jerseys working: carrying loads of wood, then cutting weeds with a machete, then sweeping the floors. But their gloves were always with them and, at each break, they played catch.

I am not against children working, but a full day of that kind of work seemed a bit much, and I wondered what their father was doing. I found him in the village, sitting in the shade outside their neat house, using a machete to whittle at a piece of wood.

When he noticed me watching, all he said was, "Thank you . . . thank you very much," then looked away, not holding my eyes.

Bosco, one of us finally realized, does not work on the island, he is a regular guest. The twenty-two-foot panga with its fancy 48-horsepower Yamaha is his, brought to fish. One evening, while I was writing at the desk in the art gallery, he stopped to see what I was doing, and we began to talk as best we could, for neither of us knew the other's language well.

I asked him his full name and, by way of explanation, he struggled with the small keys of my typewriter and wrote: "Yo soy poeta artesano y revolucionario entre otras cosas, pescador galardonado con el premio de poesía joven leonel. Miembro de la comunidad de solentiname y teniente coronel en servicio activo."

So Bosco, whom I took to be a cheerful hotel employee, was really an army colonel, and a poet as well. It clearly pleased him that I was impressed, and he invited the Americans and the Brit to fish with him the next morning.

With us went Freddie. Freddie, I also finally realized, was the colonel's fishing guide. But it was the colonel who ran the boat, steering us to a section of open lake, then anchoring not far from Padre Island, where the wild monkeys lived. I expected to fish the roots and snags along the shoreline, but Freddie and the colonel clearly knew what they were doing and, on the first cast, landed a nice guapote. The guapote is a strong fighting freshwater fish, but there could be no doubt that there were also big saltwater fish in the lake. I had already measured three snook, a popular saltwater game fish, taken in nets, that weighed nearly thirty pounds each. Yet there is a sense of infirmity in the waters of the lake—or perhaps I can't disassociate these healthy vertebrates from the sewage that I saw bubbling into the waters wherever there was a settlement. Sitting in the stern, watching us fish, Al told us of a massive chemical spill he had heard about caused, he started to say, by U.S. industrialists. But one of us had had enough of his strong politics, and cut him short: "Knock it off!" Meaning he should save it for the next solidarity meeting.

Freddie and the colonel continued to land fish and, while they fished, one of us noticed a large guapote drifting toward us, tail breaching the surface. Freddie tried to net it but missed, and I was glad for we certainly would have eaten the sick creature for supper. Though I did not see it myself, I had talked to people who had seen fish ill with ulcers, poached by cancers, and I did not doubt it. All the poverty of Nicaragua flowed into this place, and, as beautiful as the lake is, it has the same stricken quality that pervades the entire nation.

"If they ever were here, they must be gone now," one of us said finally. Meaning the sharks. The commotion of all the fish we were catching would have certainly attracted them, yet Freddie, who had grown up on the lake, was still eagerly jumping into the water to retrieve snagged lures.

No sharks? I disagreed. Nicaragua has a long history of attracting and enduring predators. Plus, intercourse between the lake and sea implied not just a historical link between political outrages, it suggested a biological resolve as well. The sharks were certainly still there.

The baseball diamond on Mancarron Island is on the highest plateau of cultivated land, higher than either the village or the small hotel. Though the field goes unused for long periods, its base paths are marked by generations of wear. The backstop is chicken wire stretched over gray planks. The field is seeds and wild flowers that catch the wind and show their milky undersides, yellow and violet. The flowers grow among cow pies and shards of pottery and glass—human spore accumulated through decades of small comings and goings. There is no fence. The outfield slopes toward the water. It is a nice part of the island, a crossing place for parrots and egrets. From the pitcher's mound you can see the lake and, beneath the blue silhouettes of volcanoes, the solitary shapes of dugout canoes: fishermen at work.

The Sharks of Lake Nicaragua

On my last day on Mancarron, I walked up to the field and watched boys playing baseball. Ramón and Juan, in the jerseys my sons had worn, were easy to recognize. As was their father, standing at the backstop with the chunk of wood he had been carving.

It was now a bat.